THE GILL HISTORY OF IRELAND

General Editors: JAMES LYDON, PH.D.
MARGARET MACCURTAIN, PH.D.

Other titles in the series

GAELIC and GAELICISED IRELAND

in the Middle Ages

Kenneth Nicholls

GILL AND MACMILLAN

Published by
GILL AND MACMILLAN LTD
2 Belvedere Place
Dublin 1
and in London through association with the
MACMILLAN
Group of Publishing Companies

Cover design by Cor Klaasen
Illustration: Ghent, University Library, MS.2466

7171 0561 X

Printed and bound in the Republic of Ireland by the
Book Printing Division of Smurfit Print and Packaging
Limited, Dublin

Foreword

THE study of Irish history has changed greatly in recent decades as more evidence becomes available and new insights are provided by the growing number of historians. It is natural, too, that with each generation new questions should be asked about our past. The time has come for a new large-scale history. It is the aim of the Gill History of Ireland to provide this. This series of studies of Irish history, each written by a specialist, is arranged chronologically. But each volume is intended to stand on its own and no attempt has been made to present a uniform history. Diversity of analysis and interpretation is the aim; a group of young historians have tried to express the view of their generation on our past. It is the hope of the editors that the series will help the reader to appreciate in a new way the rich heritage of Ireland's history.

JAMES LYDON, PH.D.
MARGARET MACCURTAIN, PH.D.

Contents

Part II: Historical

Preface

THIS book consists of two distinct parts. The first section is devoted to a general account of the society and institutions of Gaelic and gaelicised Ireland during the later middle ages, so far as the available evidence permits us to reconstruct them. The available materials on the economic condition of the country are unfortunately so scanty that no adequate picture can be drawn and I have designedly left aside literature and art, partly from considerations of space but principally because these aspects, unlike the political and legal structure, have been already the subject of a considerable degree of published work. Some other sections, especially on the Church, have been regretfully omitted due to exigencies of space: I hope to publish some of this material elsewhere. The second portion of the work consists of a brief history of those regions of Ireland outside the control of the English administration during the same period.

Both sections of this work, with the exception of a few short paragraphs on specialised matters, are based almost entirely on original research, largely among unprinted sources, a fact which creates a number of problems for a work of a popular nature without footnotes or critical apparatus.

If one might coin an epigram, Gaelic Ireland in its later period has been as unfortunate in its historiography as it was in its history. Not only has there been a destruction of source material perhaps unparalleled in western Europe, when one adds to the destruction of the Irish Public Records in 1922 the destruction of private archives which has continued unabated down to the present day, but the subject itself, the history and institutions of Gaelic Ireland during its latest period, has been left almost entirely untouched by those who have concerned themselves with the history of Ireland. A few schematic generalisations, grounded not in research on the sources but on deductions from the conditions of an earlier age, have too often been the substitute for a detailed investigation of the actual society itself. That neither the society and institutions of late medieval Ireland nor the individual history of the various regions has up to now been the subject of a work of scholarly value might seem surprising to anyone un-acquainted with the limitations of Irish historiography, especially when he notes that what seemed to have been a promising beginning had been made in the early and mid-nineteenth century. The explanation must be sought in a number of causes, not all of them in the world of learning, but certainly a most important factor in this neglect was the dichotomy which developed – and still exists in Ireland – between the fields of historical and Celtic studies.

The present work could therefore be described in the words used – with infinitely less justification than in the present instance – by Professor Otway-Ruthven to describe her *History of Medieval Ireland*, as an 'interim report' on my work on Gaelic and Gaelicised Ireland, its society and institutions. The popular work has in this case come before the learned monograph; for the defects which must necessarily arise from this inversion of the normal order, as well as for the imbalance which considerations of space have imposed in certain parts, I beg the reader's forbearance.

May I express my gratitude to the editors of this series and to my publishers Gill and Macmillan for their patience in bearing the many delays which I have inflicted on them in the production of this book, and to Dr Gearoid Mac Niocaill, who drew my attention to some slips in my original draft of Chapters II and III.

Crown copyright material quoted in this work appears by permission of the controller of Her Majesty's Stationery Office.

K. W. NICHOLLS
Paulbeg Cottage
Shillelagh

July 1971

Part I

Society and Institutions

IRELAND circa 1255

Autonomous Gaelic areas /////
Boundary of 'The Five Cantreds' ─── ?

Inishowen

Derry
O Cahan
ULSTER

Cinéal Conaill
O Donnell

Cinéal Eóghain
O Neill

Fermanagh

Armagh
O Haddy
MacMahon
O Hanlon

O Rourkes

O Reilly

CONNACHT

O Connot
O Farrell

MEATH

O Flaherty
Tuam

Athlone

Dublin

Athenry

O Molloy

O Brien

LEINSTER

Limerick

MUNSTER

Waterford

MacCarthy

Cork

0 ──────── 80 Km
0 ──────── 50 Mls

2

1 Introduction: The Background of late Medieval Ireland

Ireland has suffered in its historiography through its geographical position. At the western extremity of Europe, Ireland – so far as the native Gaelic world was concerned – was yet outside the typical European social milieu, and its analogies must in many ways be sought outside western Europe. To take a glaring example, Christianity in medieval Ireland never seems to have really expanded outside the purely religious sphere of life. In this respect Ireland may be compared – the comparison does not originate with me – with another land at the extremity of Christendom, Abyssinia. There, likewise, Christianity does not seem to have been more than a religion, whereas in the remainder of Christendom, both Latin and Orthodox, it became a whole social system. In Ireland and in Abyssinia alike, to take the most notorious example, marriage and divorce remained secular affairs, determined by secular rules quite different from the teachings of the Church on these matters. Again, the principle of the expanding clans, vital to an understanding of medieval Ireland, has no analogy elsewhere in Europe (I need hardly say that in this statement I am ignoring the other Celtic lands of Wales and the Scottish Highlands, of which the latter were in fact an integral part of the Gaelic Irish world) although parallel phenomena can be observed in many parts of Asia and Africa where, as in Ireland, the system of lineages prevailed.

It has been customary to depict medieval Ireland as

sharply divided into two worlds, the test of division being whether the ruling family in a particular area was of pure Gaelic or of Anglo-Norman origin. In fact it was not so. If we leave aside the Pale, where conditions might be said to have approximated to those of the northern border counties of England, the cultural picture of later medieval Ireland was very much the same, varying only in degree. If the Gaelic lordships of Ulster, remote from foreign influence, had retained the greatest degree of resemblance to conditions before the invasion of 1169, those of Munster were very different. If throughout the Anglo-Norman areas of Munster law and custom were a mixture of Irish and English forms and the rule of primogeniture was still generally but not invariably observed, the lordships of Anglo-Norman descent in Connacht and Westmeath would to an outside observer have appeared indistinguishable from their purely Gaelic neighbours, with whom they practised succession by tanistry and inheritance of land by 'Irish gavelkind'. The notion that late medieval Ireland was sharply divided on the basis of the national origin of the ruling groups is one which cannot survive an investigation of the actual facts.

It must be borne in mind that Gaelic and Gaelicised Ireland of the later middle ages was far from being a static society. While the basic framework of custom and institutions remained the same, the actual personnel of society was constantly changing as the clans multiplied or diminished, rose or fell in political – and therefore social – position. As the stronger lineages increased and the weaker died away or sank into the peasantry the pattern in any particular area changed accordingly. In addition, throughout the fifteenth and early sixteenth centuries the marcher areas saw a gradual replacement of the surviving English institutions by Gaelic ones, a trend that did not begin to be reversed until after 1534, while the sixteenth century was to see what appears to have been a general increase in

4

violence everywhere, leading to a decline in material conditions and economic life.

The land

Gerald of Wales describes Ireland, at the close of the twelfth century, as a land full of woods, bogs and lakes, and for most of the country, and especially the midland plain and the north, the description would still have been true in the sixteenth century. In the areas where Anglo-Norman colonisation had been dense, however, the majority of the level and good ground had been cleared for cultivation during the thirteenth century, and by the sixteenth century the counties of the Pale were almost treeless, while clearing had also taken place on a small scale throughout the period in the Gaelic areas; Paul Mac Murry, prior of Saints' Island in Lough Ree, who died in 1394, is recorded in his obit as the man who cleared Doire na gcailleach (Derrynagallagh, County Longford) and Doire Meinci (two woods, as the first element in their name, *doire*, shows) for his priory. Of more importance than deliberate clearance, however, once the first great period of settlement was over, must have been the prevention of natural regeneration by heavy grazing. English writers of the sixteenth century note the absence in most parts of Ireland of good high timber suitable for shipbuilding; the Desmond Survey of 1586 records that the woods of north Kerry consisted of 'underwood of the age of fifty or sixty years, filled with doted [i.e. decayed] trees, ash-trees, hazels, sallows, willows, alders, birches, whitethorns and such like'. But in many areas, such as the counties of Wicklow and Wexford – where in the sixteenth century there existed an important export trade in ship-building timber as well as in the pipe-staves which were to be so important an article of Irish commerce in the first part of the seventeenth century – there were still large stands of good oak timber. Woods of Scots fir were also to be found in some mountainous areas, such as the Curlews, in spite of the assertions of some modern writers to the contrary, and an English writer of 1600 notices the yew woods along the rivers of County Cork. The great destruction of the Irish woods dates largely from the seventeenth century; Boate, writing in 1654, records that many areas well wooded in 1600 had been already completely cleared by his time, and the Strafford Survey map of the barony of Athlone in County Roscommon, where in 1570 a mapmaker had recorded the presence of extensive forests of 'great oaks and much small woods as crabtree, thorn, hazel, with such like' shows that by 1637 the woods in this area, although still extensive by later standards, were confined to the rocky and broken ground unsuitable for agriculture and to the islands in the bogs.

In general it could be said that fifteenth and sixteenth-century Ireland was extensively wooded in all mountainous areas, even those of the western seaboard – with the exception, no doubt, of such regions as the Burren of County Clare – and on the margins and islands of the bogs of the central plain. Notable in this respect were the 'gallery forests' which occupied the strips of dry ground lying along the rivers of the bog country, such as the Barrow and the Suck. Another extensive area of woodland, already referred to, was that which covered northern Wexford and the adjacent regions of Wicklow and Carlow. The woods provided a habitat for the goshawks for which Ireland was renowned in the sixteenth century, although they were already becoming scarce – with the clearing of the woods in the next century the goshawk was to disappear as an Irish bird – and both woods and mountains contained large numbers of red deer, as well as the wolves which did not finally disappear until late in the eighteenth century and which made it necessary for the livestock to be brought at night into bawns or enclosures, or into the dwelling-houses themselves. It would seem that the wild pigs which were common in Gerald's time still existed in the sixteenth century, but little research has been done on the Irish fauna and flora before the transformation of the landscape, and even such an important source as the natural history of Philip O Sullivan, written about 1630, still remains unpublished.

The absence of hedges and fences in the Irish countryside is remarked upon by such writers as Spenser, and in most regions enclosed fields seem to have been almost unknown. They existed, however, in parts of such old and densely settled regions as County Kilkenny, while in the areas where stone was abundant the stones cleared from the ground to facilitate cultivation must have been piled into dividing walls, as they had been since neolithic times and still are today. Nevertheless, the normal Irish practice was to enclose the ploughed and sown areas with temporary fences made out of branches and other wood, and then to use the materials of these temporary fences for fuel during the winter months. The supply of materials for these temporary fences must itself have been a heavy drain upon the woodlands. Permanent banks or ditches were, however, common as boundaries between adjacent townlands, even in some Gaelic areas, while gardens and orchards, where these existed, would, of course, have been surrounded by earthen banks and hedges. A feature which must be noted in the lowlands was the number of lakes, remarked on by Gerald. Many of these which are known from sixteenth and seventeenth-century maps and records have since been drained, or more often converted into bogs by natural processes. On the subject of roads and tracks information seems almost non-existent. An interesting reference of 1475 mentions the highway leading from Barry Oge's country into that of Mac Carthy Reagh as having been blocked by 'walls and ramparts and great ditches' on account of the war between these two areas.

Stone bridges were fairly common in Anglo-Norman areas and are occasionally heard of elsewhere.

Ireland a lineage society

Medieval Ireland was, of course, a society of clans or lineages – referred to as 'nations' in contemporary English terminology, and the most outstanding feature in the Gaelicisation of the Anglo-Norman settlers is the speed with which, within the first century following the invasion, the concept of the clan had become established among them. Irish scholars of the present day show a curious dislike of the word 'clan', itself an Irish word (*clann*, lit. 'children', 'offspring'), but as the term is in normal use by social anthropologists to denote the kind of corporate descent-group of which I am speaking, I have no hesitation in employing it. The study, however, of clan- or lineage-based societies – which, whether in Medieval Ireland, in Asia or Africa, constitute a particular form of organisation with distinctive features in common – is comparatively recent. It would seem that until recently researchers were unwilling to accept the reality of the claims of common descent which constitute the basic qualification of a clan. In the sense in which I am using it here, a clan may be defined as a unilineal (in the Irish case, patrilineal) descent group forming a definite corporate entity with political and legal functions. This latter part of the definition is an important one, for the functions of the clan in a clan-organised society lie entirely in the 'politico-jural' and not in the 'socio-familial' sphere; that is to say, they are concerned with the political and legal aspects of life and not with those of the family.[1] Normally a clan will occupy and possess a particular territory, its occupation or ownership of the land being one of its most important corporate functions. (This does not, it need hardly be said, imply that the territory was held in common among the members of the clan or that outsiders would not be present within

8

the clan territory. The objection of some modern Irish scholars to the concept of the clan may owe its origin to a reaction against absurdities of this kind.) As the clan is a corporate entity with functions only in particular spheres and aspects of life it is, of course, absurd to conceive of a clan-based society as being *divided* into clans as if into compartments; the clan, like a modern company, can be a very variable thing. A clan may be represented by a single individual only, the only member remaining of his descent-group, which nevertheless continues to exist so long as any member of it survives. The smaller descent-groups within a larger clan may each constitute entities or clans, while remaining part of the larger one, and may again be similarly subdivided themselves.

In the case of Ireland, the greater part of the humbler classes certainly did not belong to any recognised clans or descent-groups other than their immediate family groups (father and sons, or a group of brothers). In the case of persons like these, devoid of political influence or property, the clan would have had no functions which could serve to hold it together. Conall Mageoghagan, writing in 1627, refers contemptuously to persons of this sort as 'mere churls and labouring men, [not] one of whom knows his own great-grandfather.' The phrase is significant; in a lineage-based society the keeping of genealogies is of primary importance. Not only is membership of the clan conferred by descent, but the precise details of this descent may determine a person's legal rights in, for instance, the property of the clan. In Ireland the keeping of genealogies was entrusted to the professional families of scribes and chroniclers. In 1635 we find a genealogy of the Butlers of Shanballyduff in County Tipperary prepared by Hugh Oge Magrath 'out of the new and old books of his ancestors written in the Irish language', and in 1662 Arthur O Neill, about to be admitted as a knight of the Order of Calatrava in Spain and asked for his pedigree, referred the Order to 'the chronicler Don Tulio Conrreo', otherwise Tuileagna O Mulconry, who duly produced the required pedigree back to Donnell of Armagh, King of Ireland in 976.

As the clan was a unit only in a legal and political sense, one must not, of course, expect it to show the sort of internal solidarity one expects of the family. Indeed, causes of tension and conflict might be expected to be highest within the lineage group, where rights over the clan property would be a constant ground for dispute. When we read in an early seventeenth-century pleading, with reference to two Purcell brothers who held in common a minute property in County Tipperary, that 'the said Patrick was killed by the said Geoffrey for some difference betwixt them about the said land', we see what must have been a common outcome of fraternal tension. Where the succession to a great lordship was at stake, violence of this kind would be even more likely and cousins, whose interests would normally be in direct opposition, would be almost automatic enemies. The clan might close its ranks against an outsider and collectively seek vengeance against the slayer of one of its members, but within itself it might exist in a permanent state of hostility and division. Such hostility, if continued over generations, would inevitably lead to its division into separate fragments, each of which would function as a separate clan, and the more numerous the clan, the sooner was this likely to happen.

The expanding clans

One of the most important phenomena in a clan-based society is that of expansion from the top downwards. The seventeenth-century Irish scholar and genealogist Dualtagh Mac Firbisigh remarked that 'as the sons and families of the rulers multiplied, so their subjects and followers were squeezed out and withered away' and this phenomenon, the expansion of the ruling or dominant stocks at the expense of the remainder, is a normal feature in societies of this type. It has been observed of the modern Basotho of South Africa that 'there is a constant displacement of commoners by royals [i.e. members of the royal clan] and of collateral royals by the direct descendants of the ruling prince'[2], and this could have been said, without adaptation, of any important Gaelic or Gaelicised lordship of late medieval Ireland. In Fermanagh the kingship of the Maguires began only with the accession of Donn Mór in 1282 and the ramification of the family – with the exception of one or two small and territorially unimportant septs – began with the sons of the same man. The spread of his descendants can be seen in the genealogical tract called *Geinealaighe Fhearmanach*[3]; by 1607 they must have been in possession of at least three-quarters of the total soil of Fermanagh, having displaced or reduced the clans which had previously held it. The rate at which an Irish clan could multiply itself must not be underestimated. Turlough *an fhíona* O Donnell, lord of Tirconnell (died 1423) had eighteen sons (by ten different women) and fifty-nine grandsons in the male line. Mulmora O Reilly, the lord of East Brefny who died in 1566, had at least fifty-eight grandsons. Philip Maguire, lord of Fermanagh (died 1395), had twenty sons by eight mothers, and we know of at least fifty grandsons. Oliver Burke of Tirawley (two of whose sons became Lower Mac William although he himself had never held that position) left at least thirty-eight grandsons in the male line to share his lands. Irish law drew no distinction in matters of inheritance between the legitimate and the illegitimate and permitted the affiliation of children by their mother's declaration (see Chapter IV), and the general sexual permissiveness of medieval Irish society must have allowed a rate of multiplication approaching that which is permitted by the polygamy practised in, for instance, the clan societies of southern Africa already cited.

Within a century of the invasion of 1169, the concept of the lineage or clan seems to have been already established among the descendants of the original settlers. It is perhaps significant, however, that it first appears in those whose founders had come in the original immigration from south Wales, and it is possible that the infusion of Welsh blood and ideas had prepared the way for the acceptance of the Irish system. Before the end of the thirteenth century we find a great magnate like Richard de Burgo, earl of Ulster, engaging himself as surety for 'the felons of his name'. In 1310 the concept received formal recognition in an Irish statute which decreed that the chief of every 'great lineage' should be responsible for its members, a principle which was already in force in Hiberno-English law as regards the native Gaelic clans, but which was now formally extended to those of Anglo-Norman origin. By this date many of these foreign clans had multiplied themselves in the usual Irish fashion; in 1317 a general pardon granted to various persons in County Cork included sixty-three members of the family of de Caunteton (afterwards Condon) and no less than a hundred and eleven of that of Roche. Both these families, it is interesting to note, were of Pembrokeshire origin and belonged to the original Cambro-Norman connection. The Roches were also a numerous clan in other counties besides Cork, such as Wexford, Kilkenny and Limerick, by this date.

The Anglo-Norman settlements and their decline

It would be difficult to assign an optimum date, in purely territorial terms, to the Anglo-Norman settlement in Ireland, but perhaps the last decade of the thirteenth century could be taken as such. By this date, however, the frontier in what is now County Longford was being pushed rapidly back by a succession of able chiefs of the O Farrells, while a considerable area in west Cork and

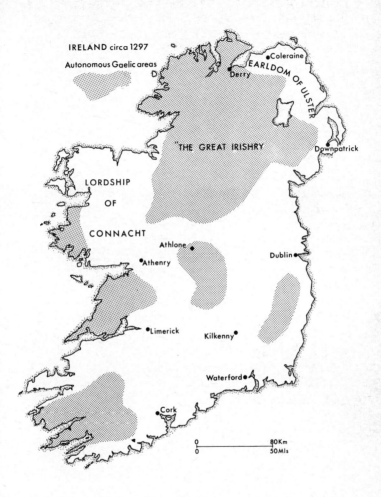

IRELAND circa 1297

Autonomous Gaelic areas

Coleraine

EARLDOM OF ULSTER

Derry

"THE GREAT IRISHRY

Downpatrick

LORDSHIP

OF

CONNACHT

Athlone

Dublin

Athenry

Limerick

Kilkenny

Waterford

Cork

0   80Km
0   50Mls

south Kerry which had been effectively occupied in the first half of the century had been lost ever since the battle of Callan (1262). On the other hand the last quarter of the century saw the occupation of eastern Thomond by the de Clares and the expansion of the de Burgo earldom of Ulster along the coast of County Derry and into Inishowen. Throughout the height of the conquest a vast area of Ulster west of the Bann, in Brefny (Counties Cavan and Leitrim) and in northern Roscommon remained in uninterrupted Irish possession, although in the first half of the century some tentative occupation, accompanied by land-grants in the area, had been made on its frontiers and such great Anglo-Norman lords as the de Verdons of Meath and the de Burgo earls of Ulster drew more or less substantial tributes from their Irish neighbours over whose lands they claimed rights, as did the Crown from the royal O Connors of Connacht in the small area left to them. This great independent area was referred to in contemporary records as 'the Great Irishry' – *magna Irecheria*. Elsewhere in Ireland, except for western Thomond, some parts of the west Connacht seaboard and – after the battle of Callan in 1262 – the extreme south-west, the free Irish remained as an independent force only in a few pockets of wooded mountain or bogland, the most extensive being centred on the mountains of Slieve Bloom and embracing the great wooded and boggy area to their north.

Over the greater part of the south and east of Ireland, and in most of Ulster east of the Bann, the colonisation had taken place in depth and a solid structure of village communities had been established. These usually had either a manorial or some sort of borough organisation – the number of these 'rural boroughs' was very great in the south – and were peopled either by a peasantry of English descent or by Irish – usually unfree betaghs – who had been effectively absorbed into the feudal and manorial system. There were a few cases of Gaelic Irish retaining their social position as feudal landowners. A rather different case is that of the O Neills of County Tipperary, an important pre-conquest clan who managed to retain a small territory near Carrick-on-Suir, in an area otherwise completely taken over by settlers. Such was, however, an exceptional instance. In most cases native Irish landowners disappeared completely from the well-settled areas, and only remained in the wooded and mountainous areas which had been imperfectly subdued. Here their position would appear to have varied. The 1305 survey of Ely O Carroll, for instance, does not mention a single O Carroll and the only Gaelic free tenants who occur in it were a group of fourteen of the O Banan family, who held two carucates (say 500 acres) between them, but within forty years the entire territory had been recovered by the O Carrolls, who must consequently have been still present in the neighbourhood at least. By contrast, the survey of Imaal (which is of about the same date as that of Ely) shows a number of O Tooles as free tenants, and not long after we find the O Mores of Leix as the recognised tenants of a considerable part of that territory under its Mortimer lords. In general, however, the Irish must have occupied the position of tenants-at-will, probably largely as pastoralists, and only rarely obtained from the new lords the charters of enfeoff-ment which would give them a legal title to the land.

In Connacht the settlement, which did not really get under way until after 1235, was of a rather different character. Although almost the entire area of the de Burgo lordship, and the southern half of the 'five cantreds' reserved to the king, had been granted out in fiefs and landholdings, there seems to have been no settlement in depth outside the commercial boroughs and their im-mediate neighbourhood – 'rural boroughs' of the kind so common in the south of Ireland would appear to have been absent – and the humbler type of agricultural settler seems not to have established himself. It is probable that almost everywhere in Connacht the native Irish remained as actual occupiers of the land under the new lords.

When we come to deal with the question of the 'Gaelicisation of the Normans' we must not forget that this expression is a misleading one. A large proportion of the members of the Anglo-Norman lineages which came into existence in the century and a half which followed the invasion were the sons of native Irish mothers. Although its extent has been underestimated by modern writers, inter-marriage between the two races was common from the beginning. Thomas fitz Maurice, son of the con- quistador Maurice fitz Gerald and ancestor of the house of Desmond, married an Irishwoman called Sadhbh, while his kinsman Richard de Carew (died 1201), who inherited Robert fitz Stephen's half of the 'kingdom of Cork', married Raghnailt, daughter of Mac Carthy. At a later date the wife of Richard de Bermingham, baron of Athenry and victor over the Irish in a famous battle there in 1316, was a Gaelic Irishwoman, as her name, Finola, shows. De Bermingham's co-victor in the same battle, Sir William Liath de Burgo, was also the husband of a Gaelic wife. But besides intermarriage the upper strata of the settlers must have had a large number of children by Irish mothers outside marriage, and it is interesting to note that it seems never to have been questioned that the children of such unions were entitled to the privileges of English status at law. According to a late tradition which, however, is hardly likely to be totally without foundation, the four houses of the White Knights, the Knights of Glin and Kerry, and the Fitz Geralds of Ardnagragh in County Kerry descended from the four sons of John fitz Thomas – son of the Thomas fitz Maurice and Sadhbh mentioned above – by the wives of four Irish chiefs under his authority. The children of such unions, although members by birth of a great Norman lineage and privileged as such, would have been brought up by their mothers in a purely Gaelic milieu. To such a background belonged a man like Sir William Liath de Burgo mentioned above, cousin of the earl of Ulster but son of a Gaelic Irishwoman (an O Connor) and husband of a Gaelic Irishwoman (an O Brien). Such a man would have been equally at home in both worlds, and it is easy to see how his descendants, given the political circumstances of their time, would pass over entirely into the Gaelic one. To speak of the 'Gaelicisation of the Normans' as if it were an external process, without taking into account the fact that many – perhaps most – of the people in question belonged by birth as much to one race as to the other, is to place the process of assimilation in a false perspective.

The Gaelic reconquest

In the areas to which it extended, the Gaelic reconquest of the fourteenth century swept away entirely the manorial system and its village settlements. A borough like Roscommon might temporarily hold out against the tide and manage to survive for some thirty years after the disappearance of English rule in the surrounding area, but in the end it was engulfed and disappeared, and – with one or two exceptions – only in a few episcopal towns did any urban settlements survive in the areas of purely Gaelic rule. (The port of Sligo was an exception, while some sort of town grew up under the O Reillys at Cavan in the sixteenth century.) If we may judge from the example of Annaghmore in County Clare, where, after the manor had passed from the de Burgos to the Gaelic Mac Namaras in the mid-fourteenth century, the latter expelled the native betaghs to replace them by their own followers, the Irish unfree population in the reconquered areas may not have benefited from the change, although some of them may perhaps have been able in the confusion to improve their status. In general, however, the land-owners who emerged in these areas after the reconquest were not the actual descendants of the pre-Norman holders but the members of the newly expanding lineages, either Gaelic lineages who had managed to keep their independence in the forests and mountains of the borders, or the lineages of 'Gaelicised Normans'. Dualtagh Mac Firbisigh remarks that although Brian O Dowda (died 1354) recovered Tireragh from the English, few if any of its former chieftains got back their hereditary lands, but 'the sons, grandsons and great-grandsons of Brian divided the land among themselves', and this would have been the normal pattern.

Although the Bruce invasion of Ireland in 1316 ended in defeat for the invaders and their Irish allies, the royal government seems never to have subsequently recovered the control of the country which it had possessed before the invasion, and the recovery of many areas by the Irish, for instance of Uí Maine by the O Kellys, certainly dates from this precise time. Thereafter the area in which the King's writ ran in Ireland began rapidly to contract. Connacht was in effect lost after 1347, although some control was retained for a period over the episcopate and clergy of the province and nominal sheriffs of Connacht continued to be appointed throughout the fifteenth century. In the second half of the fourteenth century the border areas of Westmeath similarly passed out of the government's control, their Anglo-Norman clans – Dillons, Daltons, Delamares and Tyrrells – becoming completely Gaelic. The degree to which the Daltons had by 1393 become an Irish clan like their Gaelic neighbours can be seen from the account of their doings in the following decade which is to be found in the local annals of Saints' Island[4], and even more graphically illustrated in 1414, when after the poet Niall O Higgin had been plundered by the Lord Lieutenant Stanley, Henry Dalton 'attacked the son of James Tuite and the King's subjects' and took from them the equivalent of the stock which O Higgin had lost, which he delivered to the latter. It is worthy of remark that not only do we find Dalton as the protector of that sacred personage of the Gaelic order, a poet, but that the annalist obviously did not class him among 'the King's subjects'. After the fall of Richard II the royal justices ceased to sit in Munster, which was abandoned to its local lords, although Gaelicisation in these areas was never complete; primogeniture, for instance, remained the normal rule of succession. In Munster and in County Kilkenny during the later medieval period, the law and social structure were a mixture of English and of Gaelic law, in which the former was gradually and insidiously being replaced by the latter. An important strategic factor in the loss of control by the government in the south must have been the occupation by the Mac Murroughs of the area between Carlow and the Kilkenny border, with a consequent interruption of everyday communication, although, of course, an earl of Ormond coming to Dublin would have found no difficulty in passing. Interference by the Dublin adminis-tration in the affairs of County Kilkenny, while not unknown, seems to have been fitful and of little effect during the fifteenth century and the area was administered by the Ormonds along with their liberty of Tipperary. In these Ormond territories the English element remained much stronger than in those controlled by the earls of Desmond, while the degree of Gaelicisation seems to have gone furthest in the small lordships of County Cork. In such areas, however, the manorial and village communities probably survived – as they certainly did in Tipperary and Kilkenny – through most of the fifteenth century, after which a rapid process of decay set in. The small manorial freeholders disappear, their lands passing either to their lords or to the nearby gentry families, while during the sixteenth century a remarkable change takes place in the system of tenancy, the practice of letting land at a fixed rent being replaced by a system of metayage by which the crop was divided between landlord and tenant, the landlord often providing a share of the seed. The exact economic and social implications of this change are not yet certain, but it certainly reflects an increasing approximation to Gaelic conditions, for in the purely Gaelic areas such metayage systems seem to have been normal and the greater part of the cultivators may well have been in the position of share-cropping labourers, dependent on their landlords for stock, rather than of independent tenants.

2 Political Structures and the Forms of Power

The Irish lordship

A well-known report on the state of Ireland, written in 1515, begins with the declaration that 'there be more than sixty countries, called Regions, in Ireland, inhabited with the King's Irish enemies; . . . . . where reigneth more than sixty chief captains . . . . .; and every of the said captains maketh war and peace for himself, and holdeth by the sword, and hath imperial jurisdiction within his room, and obeyeth to no other person, English or Irish, except only to such persons as may subdue him by the sword'. And further on the same writer declares: 'Also, there is more than thirty great captains of English noble family, that followeth the same Irish order and keepeth the same rule, and every of them maketh war and peace for himself without any license of the king, or of any other temporal person, save to [*sic*] him that is strongest, and of such that may subdue them by the sword'. In fact, the writer's statement as to the independence of these lords is faulty to the extent that of the ninety odd names comprised in these two lists many, especially in the lists for the Munster regions, are those of petty lords and chiefs who were acknowledged vassals of others and could never, at any time, have enjoyed much freedom of independent action. Even for the larger and more important lordships the qualification expressed in the final words 'except only to such persons as may subdue him by the sword' was a real one, for few if any of these lordships were exempt on occasion from the exactions or interference of a more powerful – even temporarily more powerful – neighbour. The writer of 1515 goes on to say that 'in every of the said regions there be divers petty captains, and every of them maketh war and peace for himself, without license of the chief captain'. These petty lordships differed from the larger, their suzerains, only in size and degree, and fall equally within the definition of 'Irish lordships' or 'countries', as they were styled in the sixteenth century. Many of the treaties made by Henry VIII's Deputies, in the first stage of the reconquest were with petty vassals of this kind, but there is seldom any mention in the indentures of treaty of their subjection to greater lords, although this cannot have been in doubt. It is indeed impossible to draw the line between a small vassal lordship and a mere landed property, and we may cite in this context the remark of Sir John Davys that every landowner 'termeth himself a lord and his portion of land his country'. In 1578 Hubert Mac Carron of County Westmeath received a patent confirming him as 'chief sergeant of his nation', with possession of the demesne lands 'which of old belonged to the chief of the nation of McCaron'. At this date the total territory of the Mac Carrons amounted to perhaps 1200 acres. In some areas too the ordinary landowners exercised quasi-jurisdictional rights, such as receiving the fines imposed for bloodshed, which in other regions belonged to the 'lords of countries'.

The term 'Irish lordship' is used here to denote what in sixteenth-century English parlance was called a 'country', one of the political units which existed in Ireland. It would be wrong to say into which Ireland was divided, for the Irish lordship – like the German states of the middle ages – must not be conceived of as a closed and defined territory but rather as a complex of rights, tributes and authority.

The normal Irish term used to denote the 'lordship' or 'country' was *oireacht* (anglicised as 'Iraght', etc) which appears frequently in both Gaelic and English sources, with the twin meanings of the territory and of the people ruled by a lord – contemporaries would not have seen this as a double meaning, but as only a single one – from 1300 onwards (although one would not guess this from the nineteenth-century translations of the annals, in which the word is constantly – though variously – mistranslated). The primary meaning of *oireacht* is 'assembly' (the derivative form *oireachtas* is the later word used in this sense), and the reference was originally probably to the assembly in which the inhabitants of the territory would meet (see below). In any case, the primary reference of the word was to the inhabitants, not to the territory which they occupied. The same would apply to *pobal*, a common alternative term for the 'Irish lordship', especially in the southern half of Ireland, and which is of course the Latin word *populus*, which occurs in precisely the same sense (that of the subjects of a lord) in the treaty of 1421 between the earl of Desmond and Lord Fitz Maurice. The term *duthaidh* is sometimes used to denote the territory ruled by a lord, as distinct from its inhabitants, but can also denote landed property of any kind. In Latin the 'country' is usually styled *patria*. In early sixteenth-century deeds Lord Barry styles himself 'captain and chief both of his nation and of his country (*patria*)'. It is customary to find among modern writers the statement that the word *tuath* was used in Irish to denote the politico-territorial unit which English writers of the sixteenth century refer to as a 'country' or 'lordship', but in fact *tuath* – the early Irish term for such a unit – seems to have become obsolete in this sense soon after the Norman invasion, although it remained a common constituent element in the names of particular districts – often not constituting separate political units. The usual pre-invasion term for the ruler of a territory, *taoiseach* ('leader'), remained in use even in the sixteenth century although by that date the foreign-

23

influenced *tighearna* ('lord') was more usual. In County Cork in the sixteenth century we find the term *ceann phobail*, 'head of a pobal' (the head of a clan was called *ceann fine*, 'head of a joint-family'). In any case, however, the ruler of a territory would normally have been known simply by his surname – O Neill, Condon (*an Cundúnach*) etc. – or by his hereditary title e.g. Mac Davy More. The term *rí*, 'king', applied to many petty rulers in pre-invasion Ireland and in the two centuries following the invasion, seems to have become obsolete, except in poetic diction, before or around 1400.

The relations of an Irish overlord with his subchiefs – the 'petty captains' mentioned above – would have depended largely upon the relative strength of the parties and this, of course, would have varied at different times. O Neill, for instance, seems to have had very little control over his principal 'urriagh' (*uirrí*, i.e. sub-king), O Cahan, while a small and weak chieftaincy like that of the O Gormleys would have been completely in his power. In any case, the degree of subjection would be more likely to be expressed in informal ways than in a formal and defined relationship. Its most important feature would be the power to cess troops and other followers at will upon the vassal. When the power of overlord and vassal was not greatly disparate the relationship would naturally be more closely defined. A treaty of 1560 between O Melaghlin and Mac Coghlan defines the tribute which the O Melaghlins had been accustomed to receive from Delvin Mac Coghlan; a yearly rent of £8, 48 hours entertainment for O Melaghlin and his train every quarter of the year, and the obligation to provide 100 kerne to serve whenever required. When in 1542 Maguire agreed to become the vassal of O Donnell, he ceded to the latter half the *eric* (blood-money) for homicide paid in Fermanagh. In 1547 Brian O Connor of Offaly, as overlord of O Dunne, was entitled to a third of all the fines which O Dunne might impose within his country. Normally, the overlord had a decisive voice in the appointment of a subchief (see below) and he would usually extract a substantial payment from the person so appointed.

Less important, perhaps, than the overlord's actual rights within a subject territory would be the insidious penetration of the latter by members of the overlord's clan who acquired land within it and eventually displaced its old landholders and ruling family. In this way the important family of the O Connors of Corcomroe (County Clare) were almost entirely displaced by their O Brien overlords in the middle of the sixteenth century. So also the little lordship of the Mac Carrons in County Westmeath, already referred to, was swallowed up during the sixteenth century by their overlords, the Dillons. Down to the end of the fifteenth century the Mac Cawell chiefs of Kinelfarry in South Tyrone appear in the annals as a minor power, but then a period begins in which the family always appear as allies or followers of Donnell O Neill (Lord of Tyrone, 1498–1509) and, after him, of his sons. By 1568 the descendants of Donnell were the lords of Kinelfarry and the Mac Cawells, while still present, were reduced to insignificance.

Tanistry and inauguration

The word tanistry is an English formation from the Irish *tánaiste* (or *táiniste*), meaning second in place or position, and is used by Celtic scholars to denote the practice, authenticated in Ireland from the eighth century, by which a chief's successor, the tanist, was nominated in the lifetime of his predecessor and automatically succeeded on the latter's death. As used, however, by English writers of the sixteenth and seventeenth centuries, it has the much more general meaning of the system of succession by seniority – to the 'eldest and worthiest' – of which tanistry in the more strict sense was only a variant. In the later medieval period it was customary for a tanist to be nominated, and in many cases certain lands and rents were attached to the office of tanist, as to the chieftaincy itself; in the case of the Mac Dermots of Moylurg a large portion of the territory bore the name of Tanistagh, and was the peculiar preserve of the tanist. The presence of a tanist was not, however, universal; and frequently it happened that the nominated tanist did not in fact succeed, being ousted by a stronger contender.

The weakness of the whole system was, of course, the conflicts which inevitably arose over the succession and the fact that there was normally a faction in opposition which was always ready to join with the natural enemies of its own clan. Theoretically, the chief – and the tanist – would be elected by the gentry of the territory in their assembly (see below), the choice falling upon the 'eldest and worthiest' of those qualified to succeed. In practice, more often than not, perhaps, there was a bloody conflict for the succession ending in the accession of the strongest or most unscrupulous. When this did not happen it was usually because one candidate, regardless of his seniority, was in a sufficiently strong position to take over the succession without opposition. When the Lord Deputy and Council adjudicated on the succession to the O Carroll chieftaincy in 1541 they found that the candidate best qualified by seniority, 'by the laws of the Irish', was incompetent 'to protect and rule the country', and he was accordingly passed over. The confrontation of evenly matched candidates, on the other hand, would frequently lead to the temporary or permanent division of the lordship.

Election to the chieftaincy lay within the *derbfine* group, that is to say, within the descendants of a common ancestor in four generations, so that anyone whose great-grandfather had been chief was theoretically eligible for election – although in practice, of course, very few of those so qualified could hope to aspire to the chieftaincy. In practice it often happened that if a chief was long-lived and survived all his own younger brothers, his son would qualify as the 'eldest and worthiest' at his death, thus producing a form of pseudo-primogeniture which has led modern writers to mistaken conclusions as to the existence of true primogeniture succession among such families as, for instance, the Mac Carthys Mór, where son succeeded father for six generations between 1359 and 1508, simply because no Mac Carthy Mór during that period was outlived by a younger brother, or at least by one strong or able enough to take the lordship. Four generations of O Dunnes – all called Teig – held the lordship of Iregan in succession from father to son during the sixteenth century, but the third of them in 1590 was so far from believing himself entitled to it by primogeniture that he drew up a remarkable deed in which he declared

my predecessors of the O Doines as competitors for the captainry or chiefry of Oregane, whereby often it came to pass that he obtained the name of O Doine who could win the same by stronger hand and force of arms. Whereby I the said Teige for avoiding the occasions that might hereafter nourish any such controversy amongst my own issue and posterity and seeing that according [to] the ancient custom of the said country I could not make an estate of inheritance of the said captainry to any of my sons and his heirs by lineal descent without great great inconvenience and danger to him, when the rest of my sons should perceive themselves to be put beside the name of O Doine contrary to the custom of Oregane. And considering also that there is none remaining of my nation that would seek the said captainry after me, [I have] thought good for the said considerations to make assurance of the said captainry and the manors, castles and lands belonging to it unto my sons Teige, Cormocke, Brian, Cahir and Mortogh successively by course of the eldership and seniority to succeed to the said captainry and name of O Doine during the life of every of them. It was not until 1606 that succession by tanistry was declared illegal by the common law judges in Ireland, in the famous case of the O Callaghans.

In the case of a chieftaincy subject to an overlord, the new chief would – at least in most regions – have been chosen not by his own clan but by the overlord and the assembly of the country as a whole. When Cathal Óg Mac Manus (the annalist) died in 1498 his son was chosen as Mac Manus by Maguire, the latter's tanist and the gentry of the country, both clerics and laity. The proceedings over the O Donovan chieftaincy in 1592 record that

> the custom of Carbery, where the said lordship [Clancahill, the O Donovans'] lies, is and hath been time beyond memory that the chieftain of the said country of Carbery, called Mac Carthy Reagh, and the most part of the gentry of the said country have and had the election, nominating and appointing as O Donovan for the time being of one of the best and worthiest of the said name, and signify the same by delivering a rod to the person so chosen, by the hands of the said Mac Carthy Reagh.

(The delivery of the rod was one of the essential features of the Irish rite of inauguration.) We are told that the O Donnells of Tirconnell constantly interfered in the election of their vassals, the Mac Sweeny lords of Fanad, and were accustomed to receive a gift of cows from the newly appointed chief. Mulmurry Mac Sweeny, who succeeded in 1461, was able to take advantage of the civil war then raging among the O Donnells to avoid making the customary payment. In 1528, the succession being disputed between two rival candidates, one of the contenders was installed by O Donnell but never succeeded in gaining recognition by the rival branch of the family, who on his death ten years later elected their own candidate against the will of O Donnell, with the result that the latter harried their country.

Whereas succession by tanistry was the normal rule in the 'Anglo-Norman' lordships of Connacht and Westmeath, in the Munster lordships primogeniture was still the usual practice. In this context one must beware of the occasional use of the word 'tanist' in its primary sense of the second in rank or position, without any implication of a right of succession.

The inauguration rituals of Irish chiefs are well known. They were very archaic and preserved very ancient features; the inauguration of the kings of Connacht at Carnfree (County Roscommon) was styled and was treated as a wedding of the king to the kingdom. Although in the later medieval period the coarbs (see Chapter IV) and clergy played a prominent part in these rituals, they were in fact of purely pagan and pre-Christian inspiration, another testimony to the slight penetration of Christian culture into Irish life. The inaugurations were always at some traditional sacred (pre-Christian) site, and in a number of cases the chief stood during the ceremony on a sacred stone which served that especial purpose. The O Neills of Tyrone were inaugurated standing on the 'Stone of the Kings' at Tullaghoge in Tyrone, which was broken into pieces by the Elizabethan general Lord Mountjoy in 1601. The placing of a white rod in the hands of the newly-installed chief was one of the most characteristic features of the ritual of inauguration. In the case of the O Donovans it was performed, as we have seen, by the overlord; in the case of great lords by one of their vassals. O Sullivan Mór, the most important vassal of Mac Carthy Mór, placed the rod in the hands

29

of the latter, and in 1592, on the death of the earl of Clancare, the then O Sullivan Mór was able to exercise an effective veto on the appointment of a successor. In Tirconnell, however, O Donnell was given the rod by the coarb of St Columkill at Kilmacrenan, O Freel, and the same coarb also had the right to give the rod to O Donnell's vassal, Mac Sweeny of Fanad, receiving a fee of five marks from the latter for doing so. Another characteristic part of inauguration ceremonies was the putting on of the new lord's shoe by his chief vassal. At the making of an O Connor as nominal king of Connacht at the traditional site of Carnfree in 1461 and again in 1488 we are told that Mac Dermot put on the new king's shoe, and O Cahan inaugurated O Neill at Tullaghoge likewise by putting on his shoe.

Public assemblies

The Irish custom of making 'great assemblies together upon a rath or a hill, there to parley, as they say, about matters and wrongs between township and township, or one private person and another', is well known. The brehons held their courts – or rather arbitration meetings – upon hills, and many sixteenth-century documents – awards of commissions, treaties with Irish chiefs and gentry, and the like – are expressly stated to have been made at hills. The eighteenth-century history of the O Reillys, compiled from local and family tradition, tells us that the assembly place of East Brefny was the hill of Shantemon in Castleterra Parish near Cavan, and that there the O Reillys were elected and proclaimed.

A treaty of 1566 between Macgeoghagan and the Fox (who agreed to become Macgeoghagan's vassal) refers to the customary assemblies held at Mayday and All Souls (*oireachtas samhna nó bealtaine*) and it may have been customary to hold assemblies in each territory at these traditional terms of the Irish year as well as for special purposes when required. The agreement in question provides for the assemblies of Macgeoghagan's country to be held at a place convenient for the Fox, who was to attend them along with the gentry of his country (*maithe na tíre*). Spenser, whom I have already quoted, refers to these meetings as being commonly attended by 'all the scum of the country', which suggests that even if the politically active element at these meetings were the landowners, the labouring population went along to see what was happening. Neighbours might also attend, to judge by the fact that a public assembly of the Mac Gillakellys of Kinelguary in County Galway in or around 1588, made to renew the ancient division of lands among the various branches of the name, was attended not only by 'the chief and principal men of the said sept of the Clangillakellies and [all] others of the said sept which were of any estate or ability or of any note or housekeeping' but also by the principal men of the O Heins and 'many others, the chief freeholders of the adjoining countries'.

The revenue and exactions of the lords

It may help to give a picture of the fiscal basis of an Irish lordship to quote from an account of the tributes and exactions levied by O Dunne, Lord of Iregan (the present barony of Tinnahinch, County Laois) as set out in an inquisition taken in 1607. In most of his territory O Dunne received a rent or tribute, varying slightly between one townland and another, of beeves, oats, butter and 'cakes of bread' and in some cases of wheat and either malt or beer also, as well as of money; he also had in these quarters the right to demand a day's provisions for twenty-four 'horseboys' (see Chapter IV) twice a year and in some cases to customary labour services of ploughing and reaping. In some other parts he received no such food-rents or services, but instead a payment of a penny for every acre of arable land. In certain parts of the territory, those occupied by the O Conrahys and O Mellans, he received a heriot on the death of every canfinny (*ceann-fine*) or head of a landowning clan; elsewhere in the territory he was entitled to one on the death of every landowner. It is clear from the document that there was considerable doubt as to what were O Dunne's real rights and what was mere extortion, an important distinction for legal purposes at this time although historically invalid. In the previous year (1606) the judges of assize at Maryborough had been called upon to adjudicate on a complaint made by the freeholders of the lands of Clonhein 'in the name of all the freeholders of O Doyne's country commonly called Iregane' complaining of

divers extortions exacted upon them by compulsion and coercion of distress by O Doyne their chief lord and his predecessors, as namely upon every quarter in the said country he and they would exact two milch cows or if they liked them [the cows] not then one pound for every cow; item, two pecks of summer oats for his horses, meat and drink for twenty-four horseboys in summer, and so [also] in winter. Item, 22 measures of wheat to O Donne's studkeeper. Item, meat and drink to O Donne's tailors and carpenters every Sunday and holiday throughout the year. Item, seven pair of brogues every year to O Donne's marshals and officers to be paid by every shoemaker inhabiting upon the said freeholders' lands. Item, 16 horseshoes unto O Donne yearly and 8 horseshoes to each of his horsemen of every smith dwelling upon the said freeholders' lands. Item, that O Doyne every year laid upon every freeholder all his horses twice a year at which times they were to give to every chief [i.e. war] horse 24 sheaves of oats and to every hackney 16 sheaves. Item, that O Donne customarily used at his going to Dublin or the sessions to cut, impose and levy his charges upon the freeholders' lands. Item, that he used to lay his kerne and bonnaghts upon the said freeholders for meat and drink.

It was admitted, however, that none of these exactions had been levied by the then chief since his accession soon after 1600, no doubt on account of the changed political circumstances of the times.

Of the list of O Dunne's exactions given above, the payments of brogues and horseshoes are only known from this source, but may well have been found elsewhere. The others are well known. The custom of the lord levying his travelling expenses upon the country was well known, and was no doubt theoretically justified – if such justification was ever thought necessary – by the plea that he was going on the business of the country. When the earl of Desmond travelled through any of his territories, the entire expenses of himself and his train had to be borne by the barony through which he was passing. It was also customary for the lords to force their countries to pay the expenses of any guests whom they might entertain, and in fact every kind of outgoing, as well as the support of all their servants and followers, was imposed upon their subjects instead of being paid out of their own funds. Building expenses were treated likewise. The O Dunne inquisition of 1607 refers to 'works and customs of cutting and drawing wood and timber, and also of building, repairing and keeping staunch the castles, halls and bawns belonging to O Doyne from time to time, which the jurors say was done of compulsion and not of right'. This last-mentioned service, of erecting and repairing buildings, was called musteroon and was also general. In 1534 Pierse, earl of Ossory, was accustomed to force the inhabitants of County Kilkenny to provide the masons and labourers employed on his building-works with free board and lodging, even on feast-days and holidays when they were not working, and also to cart without payment with their horses all the building materials needed.

The presentments of 1534 give perhaps the best picture of the whole system of Irish exactions in its most extreme form. The same exactions recur again in the Desmond Surveys and elsewhere under a multitude of different names. Earl Pierse of Ossory, like O Dunne, used, through his servants, yearly levy on every inhabitant of the county of Kilkenny 'another exaction for his horses called summer oats, paying nothing for the same'. He quartered his huntsmen and hounds – three packs, for deer, hares and martens respectively – on the people of the country, as other Munster lords and the earls of Kildare did on their subjects. (Kildare's hounds had to be given the same rations of butter and bread as a man.) It will be noticed that the necessary but profitless hunting of wolves and foxes was left, apparently, to the wretched inhabitants themselves. He and his family were accustomed to take cuddies (Gaelic *cuid oidhche*) or entertainment for a night for themselves and their train of attendants at the houses of the various gentry of the county. Cuddies were a universal custom, and in the case of a great lord with a large train of attendants must have amounted to a very large cost. A treaty of 1529 between the earl of Desmond and his cousin Gerald fitz John of the Decies provides that the earl is to have one such entertainment yearly in the Decies, but that he shall have with him 'not an assembly made of the neighbouring country but [only] his customary train of followers'. Cuddies, once established, were converted into a fixed charge which had to be paid whether the lord turned up to take them or not. The cuddies due to Mac Carthy Mór, if he did not turn up to collect them, had to be sent to his house in fixed proportions of meat, flour, whiskey, ale and honey, or a money payment of £4 8s 8d instead. O Dunne received, as payment instead of a cuddy, four quarters of beef with its tallow, a fat pig, 12 cronocks of wheat (a cronock was 24 quarts), 32 cronocks of malt and 13s 4d in money. The lord's officers were also entitled to certain fees from the person paying the cuddy. The cuddy was certainly of very early origin, and was not confined to a secular context; the 'noxials' which the bishops of Connacht and Ulster received from their erenaghs and (in some cases) clergy were, in fact, cuddies.

This whole system of free entertainment for the lord, his troops, servants and hangers-on, which English writers refer to under the general heading of 'coyne and livery' and the detailed aspects of which appear in the records under a multitude of different names, was the fundamental base of the Gaelic system of authority. Its oppressiveness, especially in some areas of Munster where it seems, both in purely Gaelic lordships and those of Anglo-Norman origin, to have been heaviest, must have been very great. A presentment of 1576 states that Lords Barry and Roche in County Cork were accustomed to take for their own use, instead of coyne and livery and other exactions, three quarters of the lands of every free-holder within their territories, leaving the owner the other quarter for himself free of exactions, and when we tot up the amount of exactions taken by, say, the earl of Desmond out of any given area we see that this proportion must have reflected the general situation everywhere in Munster. The commissioners of the Desmond Survey in 1585 thought that the irregular exactions of this kind taken by the earl of Desmond amounted to ten times as much as the regular chief-rents in money and cattle which he received from the freeholders – and these were far from light. In the Munster lordships it was also the custom for the lords – whether of Norman or Gaelic origin – to levy the dowries for their daughters off the country, thereby converting into a compulsory exaction the Irish custom by which neighbours and relations subscribed towards the dowry. One gets the impression that the extortions of the Munster lords were much heavier than those in the more purely Gaelic areas of the north and west, perhaps owing to the greater political stability enjoyed by the former, but one must remember that our information on the former is much greater. In Thomond, fixed rents in money would seem to have been more usual than they were elsewhere.

James, earl of Desmond (1419–56) is traditionally said to have been the first to impose coyne and livery for the kerne and galloglass on the countries under his rule, and by 1467 the abbot of Odorney in Kerry was complaining to the Pope about the exactions of the earls and of Lord Fitz Maurice, including kernety and the familiar horse-keepers, dogkeepers and the dogs themselves. The contemporary James, the 'White Earl' of Ormond, imposed kernety and galloglass upon the counties of Tipperary and Kilkenny; when he appointed his half-brother James Galda Butler as keeper of the county of Tipperary he gave him the right to take cuddy in every freeholder's house in the county. The exactions seem to have increased everywhere during the sixteenth century.

In the areas which had never known English rule in the middle ages, in Gaelic Ulster and in O Reilly's country, we find the survival of a much older system of revenue provision in the existence of a *lucht tighe* (lit. 'people of the household') or 'mensal lands', as they are called by English writers, that is to say, a special tract of territory charged with the duty of providing for the chief's household, while the remainder of the area under his rule provided soldiers and occasional cuddies. These 'mensal lands' must not be confused with demesne lands, as has been done by some writers; in Fermanagh the ballybetagh of land around Enniskillen, which Maguire 'manured [cultivated] with his own churls [labourers]', was quite distinct from his mensal lands, which yielded him a rent in butter, meal, pigs and other provisions and the greater part of which was the freehold of the Mac Manus family. In return for this rent these lands were free from the usual charges (cessing of troops, etc.) imposed on the country. It was the custom in some lordships for certain rents to be set apart by custom for the wife of the lord for the time being.

Lords' land rights

As is well known, most Irish lordships had a certain amount of demesne land attached to the office of chief, but this was not universal nor was – as has been alleged – this demesne land always clearly distinguished from the private inherited estate of the sept in which the chieftaincy was vested. The strong and important chieftaincies of the two Mac Donoghs, in County Sligo, do not seem to have had any demesne lands at all. Some other great Connacht lordships, however, possessed large lands which went with the chieftaincies.

Of more importance politically were the rights of the lord over the lands of his subjects. These mainly arose from the right of the lord, if his dues and exactions were left unpaid, to take the lands out of which they were due into his hands as a pledge for the amount owing. Justice Luttrell in 1537 refers to the practice of the marcher lords, when the lands had been left uncultivated on account of the pressures of coyne and livery, seizing them for the amount of coyne due, and the inquisition on Hugh O Kelly, the last official chief of his name, found that he died (1591) in possession of certain lands which by right belonged to the sept of the O Murrys, but which O Kelly detained by force because the O Murrys, 'being poor men, were unable to satisfy the exactions imposed on them by the said Hugh'. Lands might also be taken by the lord in pledge for a fine imposed by him. James, earl of Desmond (died 1558), seized certain lands in County

Kerry because the owner had sworn falsely on his, the earl's, hand (see Chapter III). Closely connected with these practices is that which we find in County Cork in the sixteenth century, by which landowners, finding themselves intolerably worn down by the exactions of their lords, surrendered three-quarters or more to the latter to have the remaining fragment free of exactions, an agreement which the lords did not always honour, as can be seen by the complaint of a wretched freeholder of Lord Roche to Sir Henry Sidney in 1576. Having so surrendered seven-and-a-half out of eight ploughlands which he had inherited, he found that after a short interval Lord Roche began to impose exactions on the remaining half ploughland. Sometimes, in these Anglo-Norman areas where the lords' powers seem to have been much greater than in the Gaelic, a lord would keep a freeholder in prison until he surrendered his lands. We have a record of the second earl of Clanrickard doing this with one of his near kinsmen, whom he kept seven years in prison until the prisoner signed the deed of conveyance.

Another custom apparently common was a rule by which the lord might enter upon and occupy unoccupied lands during the absence of the true owners. The O Dunne document of 1607 records a claim made to lands by a man who alleged 'that he or his ancestors left the same in the hands of O Doyne to be kept for them about 30 years since, as the manner of the country is if any freeholder depart out of the same'. In fact the lands in question seem to have been subsequently given by O Dunne to his natural son, and all these customs must have been means whereby, in the words of Sir Thomas Cusack in 1543, 'the father, being lord of the country, will extort the inferior and so by cavillations pluck from him his lands, to the intent that every of his children shall have lands and possessions'. We have an instance of the process of annexation at work in a story related in the traditional

History of the O Reillys. The district of Lower Clankee in County Cavan was held under the sept of Clann Chaoich (a branch of the O Reillys) by freeholders who paid them rents out of the lands. Connor O Reilly, a son of the John who was chief 1449–60, acquired lands in the area from the freeholders and built a castle there. His failure to pay the accustomed rents to the Clann Chaoich led to a quarrel with the latter in which he was slain, whereupon his brother Turlough (chief 1467–80) came with a large force to avenge his brother. In the end the chief of Clann Chaoich, to make peace, agreed to pay an *eric* of 1800 cows for the slain man, and pledged the whole of the rents of Lower Clankee for its payment and, as the sum was never discharged, the area remained in the possession of the sept descended from John O Reilly.

Monopolies and pre-emption

Within their territories the Irish lords claimed the right of pre-emption (*codhnachas*) and this was also adopted by the marchers. In 1537 Justice Luttrell noted that

> if any of the poor tenants of any marchers have any cow, oxhide or other victual to be sold, and sell the same to others, not offering it first to the lord owner of the soil, his said lord taketh cane [*cáin*] or penalty therefore, commonly 6s. 8d., and yet his said lord would not give therefore nothing so much as the thing may be sold for to others.

At the same period Sir William Bermingham of Carbury in County Kildare 'maketh it for a law throughout the barony of Carbre . . that no man shall [bring] any manner [of] thing that they have to any market, but only to his [Sir William's] wife, and she to make the price', and Donnell Mac Cragh 'of the Mountain' in County Waterford 'hath ordained and established that none of his tenants shall sell or buy any hides but to himself at a certain [i.e. fixed] price to his own advantage'. At the end of the century the freeholders of O Driscoll's country were bound to offer the lord the first refusal of any goods they wished to sell, though he was bound by custom to pay as much as could otherwise be obtained. It seems to have been a common practice for a lord to grant to a particular merchant or merchants – no doubt in return for some financial return – the exclusive right of trading within his country.

Lords' officers

In the thirteenth century the O Connor kings of Connacht had at least the rudiments of a 'household' i.e. administrative organisation, with a chancellor and seneschal, but in later medieval times it is impossible to discover any trace of a central administrative structure in even the largest lordships, if we except the Ormond and Desmond palatinates. Local administrative officers of course existed for the purpose of collecting the lords' rents and tributes. These were known in Irish as *maoir* (sing. *maor*) and their office was sometimes hereditary. The Knight of Kerry was the hereditary collector of the earl of Desmond's rents in that county, and received a twentieth part of them for his fee. A very important officer was the marshal (Gaelic *marasgal*), whose duty was to apportion the billeting and cessing of troops on the country. The O Donnelly family were hereditary marshals to O Neill, and the O Connellys to Mac Mahon, while the Butlers of Cahir enjoyed the hereditary marshalship of 'one half of the host' of their cousins the earls of Ormond. The marshal of an important lord would have sub-marshals under him to execute his office, for which he was remunerated by receiving a certain proportion of 'black men', that is, allowances paid for non-existent soldiers. The O Donnellys seem to have received an allowance of this kind of one in forty; they were also entitled to the heads and hides of the cattle killed to provide cuddies for O Neill by his vassals. This seems to have been a usual perquisite of the marshal. An interesting deed of 1584 records that Teig na Mainistreach Mac Carthy Mór (died 1428) had appointed one Cathal O Rourke hereditary weir-keeper of the River Laune near Killarney; now by his deed Donnell Mac Carthy Mór, earl of Clancare, confirmed to Manus O Rourke the office of weir-keeper and furthermore appointed him marshal of all his houses, setting out his fees in detail. O Rourke was to receive the heads and hides of all cattle and sheep killed to provide the cuddies due to the earl from his vassals; he was to collect and send to the earl such cuddies as the earl did not go to take up in person, 'receiving his accustomed fees'; he was to receive the hides of all beeves killed when the earl was in camp; fees from the fosterers of the earl's children; and, finally, he was to receive five marks (£3 6s. 8d.) or five horses on the marriage of any of the earl's daughters or the daughters of a future Mac Carthy Mór, to be paid by the husband on the wedding day. It is obvious that the officers of a great lord must have had rich pickings. We are expressly told in the Desmond Survey of 1584 that the earl's officers, if there happened to be no occasion to quarter galloglass in a particular district, would collect an equivalent sum from the inhabitants and pocket it themselves.

'Buyings' and sláinte

The custom of buying the protection (sláinte) of a great man was one of the most characteristic and important institutions of late medieval Ireland. The word ceannuigh-eacht, 'purchase', transliterated into English as 'kenaght' and translated as 'buying' was used in a technical sense to denote the payment made for this purpose, which entitled the payer to the protection and assistance of the person to whom it was made. It was thus in fact a late development of the ancient Irish institution of clientship.

Any injury done to the person who had so purchased protection was treated as an injury done directly to his protector, and we find recorded in the Kildare Rental Book, for example, fines of sixty or seventy cows taken by the ninth earl for the breaking of his 'slantyaght' (*slánuigheacht*) or 'slante' upon persons who enjoyed it. The long section of the Rental Book devoted to 'The Earl of Kildare's duties upon Irishmen' is almost entirely composed of rents and tributes granted to the earl 'for their defence' by persons who so wished to enjoy his protection. In 1457 we find the Daton family in County Kilkenny granting certain lands to James Butler of Ormond in return for his protection. In 1537 Justice Luttrell declares that

> in causes of contention for lands and goods in the marches betwixt parties, if any of the parties give rewards, called 'buyings', to the captains there or their sons or such other, he that accepteth such buyings taketh pledges for the same contention [of the other party] and oftentimes putteth with force him that giveth the said buyings in possession of the thing in debate.

The custom of *sláinte* cut right across the system of lordships and must have greatly restricted the power of the lords over their own subjects. It must have been greatly to the advantage of a small Irish landowner to pay even a heavy tribute to such a man as the earl of Kildare, if by doing so he was assured of freedom from the arbitrary exactions and oppressions of his own chief. This aspect of the custom seems to have been disliked by the English authorities, no doubt as reducing the effectiveness of settled authority in any area; by their treaty with the Lord Deputy in 1549 the Ulster chiefs renounced the custom of 'slantye' in any area outside their own rule, and in 1565 Sussex's proposals for reform in Ireland included one that no man was 'to give any buying to any man not dwelling within his own country'.

As well as from lesser men to the great, however, 'buyings' were also given among equals in order to secure support or assistance. In 1549 Hugh O Neill of the Fews complained that the late Mac Donnell Galloglass, since deceased, had promised him £40 'in name of a purchase, as is the custom of the Irish, that he should be a friend to him from henceforth' and asked that this debt should be paid. Mac Donnell had been seeking assistance in his war with his own lord, Conn Bacach O Neill of Tyrone.

Such payments, given between equals or by the lesser to the great, must be distinguished from another although similar kind, those known in Irish as *tuarastal*. This went back to a very ancient institution of Irish society. The acceptance of *tuarastal*, which bound the acceptor to the service of the giver, carried a definite recognition of superiority in the latter. While the amounts given for *tuarastal* were often substantial, they seem on other occasions to have been little more than honorific, their value being less important than their symbolism; in 1549 Conn Bacach O Neill gave to Maguire, to attach him to his service, eight horses, a 'jack' or tunic of quilted leather (which was used as a kind of armour) and a mailshirt. The horses which the earls of Kildare bestowed lavishly upon various persons had probably the same significance.

The word *sláinte* was also used in a somewhat different though closely allied connotation to that described above, to denote the sureties who would be called in to guarantee the observance either of a legal decision or of a treaty or contract. These will be dealt with below in the section devoted to legal forms (Chapter III).

3 The Legal System

The Irish legal system

The native Irish legal system was and is usually referred
to as the Brehon Law, from brehon, the English form of
the Irish word *breitheamh*, a judge. The early Irish law
texts, which date from the eighth and ninth centuries at
least, although they remained the subject of learned study
throughout the medieval period, had by that time ceased
to be of practical relevance to the realities of Irish society;
indeed the greatest authority on the early laws, Professor
Binchy, has gone so far as to declare that the brehons of
the late medieval period kept their study of the ancient
texts, which he describes as 'antiquarian windowdressing',
quite apart from their everyday legal work. It would seem,
however, that the ancient texts served as a source of
maxims and rules which could be used – if with little
relevance to their original context – in pleadings and
decisions. On the other hand it seems certain that Irish
law, in the later medieval period, was strongly influenced
by Roman law. In the present short survey I intend to
confine myself to what can be discovered of the actual
workings of the Irish legal system in the later middle
ages, and to the mixture of English and Irish law which
prevailed in the marcher areas. No set of enactments or
decrees by any Gaelic lord or Gaelicised magnate is
known to survive, although we know that such existed.
Owen O Reilly, lord of East Brefny (died 1449), was
remembered as having 'with lay and ecclesiastical consent

44

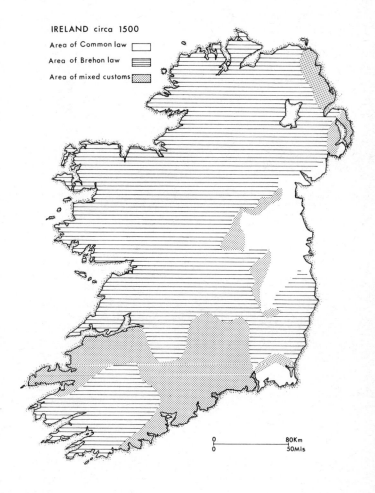

IRELAND circa 1500

Area of Common law

Area of Brehon law

Area of mixed customs

0   80Km
0   50Mls

composed the statutes by which the men of Brefny abide'. In 1433 the White Earl of Ormond promulgated at Fethard, with the consent of the archbishop of Cashel, the bishop of Lismore, and the communities of Kilkenny and Tipperary, a series of statutes for the government of these counties. Unfortunately the text has been lost and we know only the two opening clauses. The agreement which Brian Mac Mahon and the other lords of Irish Oriel entered into with the bishop of Clogher in 1297, which guaranteed the immunity of the church and its lands from exactions or violence and laid down rules for the enforcement of this protection, also belongs to the category of legislation, and there were no doubt many other examples of the same kind which have not been preserved. Justice Luttrell in 1537 refers to the lords and great men of the marches making 'penal laws upon hills to poll (tax) the poor people, and if any poor man offend that law he shall pay the penalty without any forgiveness'. Most of this type of decree would no doubt have been concerned with protecting the lord's fiscal interests.

A peculiar custom which might perhaps be referred to here was that of taking the oath upon the hand of the lord of the country. Perjury committed after such an oath would be severely punished by the lord as an insult to himself. James, earl of Desmond (died 1558), seized some lands in County Kerry because the proprietor had sworn falsely on his hand in denying the theft of certain hawks from a neighbour, and at the same period a false oath on O Neill's hand incurred a fine 'as the bishops and the best learned in the country shall adjudge, as sometimes 60 kine, and other times more'.

The judges

The Irish judges and lawyers, the brehons, like most other professional groups in Ireland, were for the most part hereditary. The most important of the families of hereditary jurists were the Mac Egans and Mac Clancys, but there were many others. In late medieval practice at least every area had its official brehon, appointed by the lord or at least recognised by him. In 1547 two Mac Clancy brehons are described as 'ordinary judges' of the territory of Comsey, in County Tipperary. In the north, these official judges seem not necessarily to have belonged to the traditional jurist families but to have been sometimes chosen from the ranks of the ecclesiastical lawyers. Art Mac Cawell, 'judge of O Neill' in 1455, was also official to the archbishop of Armagh in the deanery of Tullaghoge and to the bishop of Derry in that of Maghera; he belonged to a family of hereditary clerics, not lawyers. In the sixteenth century it seems to have been often the custom for the brehons to sit along with lay arbitrators, local lords or other notables, but it is uncertain whether this custom was of long standing; it is more likely to have been an innovation. Besides the fee which he received for his decisions, the official judge would seem also to have received a permanent retaining fee from the territory; in County Kilkenny in 1537 the brehons exacted a pig every second year from every townland.

Brehon law and English law

As during the period of the colony the Irish were considered as a separate nation outside the ambit of English law, the government had no objection to their being regulated by their own laws in their relations with each other, and indeed one aspect of the Irish legal system, the law of *cin comhfhocuis* ('kincogish') or joint family responsibility, seems to have been adopted by the administration in its relations with the Irish from the beginning. The use of Brehon law among the descendants of the settlers probably began in the first quarter of the fourteenth century. In 1351 a council held at Kilkenny by the Justiciar, Sir Thomas de Rokeby, prohibited the use of 'the law of the march and of Breawen, which are not law and ought not to be called law' by the English, a prohibition repeated by the more famous Statute of Kilkenny in 1366. In practice, of course, this, like other prohibitions against the adoption of Gaelic customs, meant nothing in the areas in which the authority of the government was slight or non-existent, and the use of the Brehon law, and of the hybrid known as march law, must have continued to spread. Without royal judges the common law could not function, and judges ceased to be appointed for either Munster or Connacht soon after 1400. The earliest definite reference which I have been able to discover to the employment of a Gaelic brehon by an Anglo-Norman magnate, however, is in a deed of the White Earl of Ormond, undated but certainly of or around 1432. By this deed the earl granted lands in County Tipperary to Donnell Mac Clancy, 'learned in the law', 'for his good service and faithful counsel in his faculty [i.e. learning] to be given to the said earl and his heirs in future'. The grant was to pass to Donnell's heirs provided they had the same faculty. An interesting clause was that Mac Clancy should be liable for any damage done to the earl's tenants by persons enjoying his hospitality or their followers. By the sixteenth century the Mac Clancys were employed as regular judges throughout the Ormond territories in Kilkenny and Tipperary. The ninth earl of Kildare was said to have used both Brehon law and English law, 'whichever he thought most beneficial, as the case did require'. In 1476 the common law was not in use in County Waterford, 'but only the wicked and damnable law called Brehon law', and the position was still the same in 1537. In Kilkenny at the latter date, while the King's writ ran in the county, the inhabitants of the latter used the Brehon law between themselves and it was also used in cases arising between them and the inhabitants of the town of Kilkenny; only in cases entirely between townsfolk was the common law used. In some western towns, such as Galway, the common law had been replaced in use not by Brehon law but by the Civil (Roman) law, which in the late fifteenth century was stated to be the only law in use in that town. In 1519 the mayor and corporation of Galway decreed that 'no Irish judge or lawyer shall plead in any man's cause or matter within our court, for it [the Brehon law] agreeth not with the King's laws nor yet the Emperor's [the Roman law] in many places', a formula which would suggest that the common law had been reintroduced in the town, but had not yet entirely displaced Roman law.

The retreat of the Brehon law began with the re-assertion of the authority of the Crown after the suppression of the Kildare rebellion. In 1538 Earl Pierse of Ossory wrote to the Lord Deputy that he had proclaimed its abolition within the liberty of Tipperary, and by 1547, when the liberty was in the King's hands through the minority of Earl Thomas, the common law was already in full force, at least in the more southern and peaceful parts. It must have disappeared from County Kilkenny by this date, but in 1548 we find the mayor of Waterford and some others, as general commissioners appointed by the Lord Deputy to settle the disputes of the Powers, awarding an *eric* (see below) for the death of one of that family. It is noteworthy that the brehon families – unlike, for instance, the bards – seem to have had little difficulty in coming to terms with the administration and even in serving it. One may instance the case of Boethius (*Baothghalach*) Mac Clancy, the well-known sheriff of Clare who died in 1588, while one of the Mac Egans of Ormond was slain on the English side at the battle of Kinsale. Certainly the administration was perfectly prepared to make use of their technical legal knowledge and even to recognise their awards in criminal and semi-criminal matters in areas which had not yet been completely subjected to the common law. In 1559 the Lord Chancellor and two judges, commissioned to arbitrate a boundary dispute between the baron of Upper Ossory and Lord Mountgarret, were ordered to join with them for the purpose four O Doran brehons, two nominated by each of the parties, and in 1592 we find Lord Deputy FitzWilliam issuing a warrant for the enforcement of a brehon decree for damages made 33 years earlier but never paid in full. A general proclamation against Brehon law had been issued by the Irish Council in 1572, but it is obvious that its enforcement was lax and we hear of awards for homicide even in the first years of the reign of James I. It is significant, however, that in the last recorded case the arbitrators, no doubt afraid of being involved in a criminal matter, afterwards disclaimed their own award.

The Irish Court of Chancery, from its establishment as a court of Equity in the time of King Henry VIII, was ready to accept and enforce Irish rules of inheritance – such as 'Irish gavelkind' and tanistry – as local customs having the force of law, although on occasion it was equally ready to abrogate such customs when they appeared to it unreasonable or inequitable, such as the rule which excluded women from inheriting land (see below). To this Court, at least during the sixteenth century, a brehon decree would constitute an arbitration which should, unless some good reason appeared to the contrary, be enforced against the party who refused to abide by it. The desire to extend its jurisdiction by taking cognizance of matters unrecognised by the common law certainly played a part in this liberal recognition of Irish custom.

Legal procedures

The decision of a brehon in a conflict between parties was in fact an arbitration, to which both parties must –

theoretically at least – have agreed to submit themselves. In practice, we can be sure that in cases where his own interest was involved – as when he was entitled to a share of the damages (see below) – the lord of the country would interfere to force an unwilling defendant to submit to arbitration, but in most private cases it would be left to the plaintiff himself to bring about this result. From this arose the practice of private distress which was one of the most characteristic features of the Irish system and one which aroused the deepest opposition on the part of English administrators, being in fact made felony by a sixteenth-century statute (which, however, admitted a number of privileged exceptions: thus the inhabitants of many of the trading towns were allowed to go on exercising it). In the absence of any official machinery to constrain a defendant to answer, the person having a claim upon him would seize upon his cattle or other goods for this purpose. There are also records of lands being seized as a 'pledge for justice'. In County Kilkenny in 1537 even priests were in the habit of taking private distresses for the fees payable to them for christenings, weddings and similar occasions. A more peculiar method of enforcing recourse to arbitration, and one which had come down from a very early period, was that of fasting upon a person. The claimant would go to the house of the person upon whom he wished to bring pressure and remain there without eating for a day and a night. In the later medieval period fasting would appear to have been largely confined to ecclesiastics. In 1365 the archbishop of Armagh, in confirming the privileges of the O Mulcallan family, hereditary keepers of St. Patrick's bell, did so on the condition that they would 'by the authority of the bell' fast upon anyone who molested his tenants. In 1530 Niall Conallach O Neill appealed to the then archbishop of Armagh against certain clerics who, he said, were disturbing him by fasting upon him and ringing bells.

Among the offenders were the same O Mulcallans, and the bells in question were of course the bells of saints which were important relics (see Chapter V). It is likely that the clerics in question were endeavouring to obtain satisfaction from Niall for extortions committed by him from their church-lands. By this time the church was losing its traditional prestige, and when in 1536 Magragh, the coarb of Lough Derg, fasted upon some other O Neills the latter retaliated with a raid in which two kinsmen of the coarb were slain.

The brehons or arbitrators would sit and give their decision in public, in the usual Irish assembly – indeed the hearing of lawsuits was the most common reason for such assemblies – upon a hill or rath. We know from some surviving examples of pleadings that the parties would at least sometimes employ pleaders or advocates, members of the jurist families who would lace their arguments with a profusion of more or less irrelevant quotations from the ancient law texts. For their decision the judges received a fee called *oiledhéag*, according to most sources an eleventh of the sum in demand or damages awarded. The enforcement of the award or decree against a recalcitrant party, in the absence of any public machinery for this purpose, must have been often very difficult, and indeed it is obvious that, even if he succeeded in bringing his opponent to accept arbitration, a poor or weak plaintiff would have little chance of obtaining redress from a powerful defendant. In order to secure enforcement of the decision it was customary, as in the case of treaties and contracts, to appoint sureties (*sláinte*), usually persons of importance who would be bound to intervene to secure observance of the terms. If lay arbitrators had taken part they might double this role with that of sureties. Another form of *sláinuigheacht* also invoked in important treaties was that of the church and the poets, the former being bound to excommunicate the party guilty of a breach of his agreement and the latter being similarly obliged to assail him with their curses (usually miscalled 'satires', see Chapter IV). A well-known treaty of 1539 between O Donnell and O Connor Sligo was guaranteed in this way, as was the deed of foundation of Lisgoole friary in 1580.

Compensation and the principle of joint responsibility

In the eyes of contemporary English observers the most striking feature of native Irish law was the absence of any system of criminal law properly so called. Theft, homicide, arson, were simple torts to be resolved by the payment of damages to the injured party, his lord or his kin. In this, of course, the Irish legal system agreed with the early Germanic codes and stood in especially sharp contrast with the severity of the medieval English law, which awarded the death penalty almost universally in criminal cases (although in actual practice this rigour was mitigated to some extent by the frequent granting of pardons as well as by such a rule as that of 'benefit of clergy'). Irish law, as such, knew no punishments. This is not to say that punishments by death or mutilation were not inflicted by the arbitrary will of rulers; we know that in fact they were, and a reference in the annals to the prompt suppression of the incipient disorder which manifested itself in Connacht after the death of King Cathal Crobhdearg (1224) suggests that the O Connor kings of Connacht may have already decreed the punishment of mutilation for various offences (a robber was punished with amputation of hands and feet, a rapist with blinding, if this is not, as has been suggested, a euphemism for castration). At a later period we read more than once in the *Annals of Ulster* of servants who had murdered their masters being put to death (by burning or hanging) and the same source records in 1500 the hanging by Maguire of a noted horse and cattle thief called Melaghlin Bradach ('the thief') O Flanagan. Accordingly to the ancient law, a person whose clan had renounced responsibility for his acts by a formal and public process became an outlaw who could be legally put to death by anyone whom he injured, and it is probable that this rule, or a modification of it, was still in force in late medieval times. Certainly we hear of wrongdoers being ordered to be handed over to the injured party if they could not pay compensation, and although it is not stated that he could deal with them as he pleased there would seem to be otherwise little point in the proviso. In any case men of humble status would have had no kindred that could afford to redeem them for their more serious crimes. In 1537 in County Waterford, an area of mixed law, 'the lord or lady taketh of the poor thief five marks, and of the rich thief more, and if he have nothing, he shall be hanged; his friends (i.e. relations) shall be warned to redeem him by a certain day, or else [he is] to be hanged.'

The *eric* (the technical term for the fine or compensation) for homicide was a heavy one; in Tirconnell around 1600 it amounted to the enormous sum, for the period, of 168 cows. In 1400 126 cows had been paid in Connacht as *eric* for a man of learning who had been accidentally slain. The sum certainly varied with the rank of the victim; in 1554 the earl of Kildare levied an *eric* of 340 cows for his foster-brother, slain by the Mac Coghlans, but here the insult to the earl's honour would have been taken into account. Certainly we hear of much smaller *erics*; in 1548 the mayor of Waterford and other arbitrators awarded 40 marks (perhaps equivalent at current rates to 50 cows) as 'sawte or erycke' for one of the Powers slain in the internal wars of that family. In the matter of homicide it would seem that in the later middle ages there entered the concept of a public offence, the greater part of the *eric* being payable not to the victim's kin but to his lord.

The account given of the practice in County Kilkenny in 1537 is that

> upon every murder committed the whole kindred of the party murdered do use to compel the whole kindred of the murderer to come before the said Irish judge, and then the judge will compel the defendants each of them to be contributors to such sum of money as shall be adjudged by him, and two parts [$\frac{2}{3}$] thereof to be paid to the principal captain of the plaintiffs, and the third part thereof to the next of the blood of the party murdered . . .

In cases of lesser injuries the lord's share would apparently be less. A case in the mid-sixteenth century shows that of seventy cows awarded as damages for some unspecified injury, fourteen were paid to Mageoghagan as lord of the country, and the remainder to the plaintiff. Such fines for homicide and other crimes must have formed an important part of the revenues of an Irish lord. A form of penalty which must be mentioned here is the fine imposed for the shedding of blood in an affray. This was probably of Anglo-Norman origin, but seems to have been universally in force in Ireland, even in purely Gaelic areas. In the termon lands of Armagh diocese the fine for bloodshed was 6s 8d, paid to the archbishop. In County Kerry the fine was only 3s 4d. The synod of Limerick in 1453 tried to decree that fines for bloodshed committed within churches should go to the bishop, not to the local lord, even if the offenders were his subjects.

Theft involved the thief in a payment of several times the value of the stolen goods. According to the invariable rule of Irish law, if stolen cattle or other goods were tracked to a man's land the owner of the land must either follow the track further or accept responsibility for the theft. This rule is found in the agreement of 1297 between the bishop of Clogher and Mac Mahon, and was enshrined as law in an ordinance of the Irish Privy Council in 1571. An interesting legal document in Irish, whose difficulties of interpretation are not lessened by the fact that it is only preserved to us in a nineteenth-century printed version, records the ruin which came to the O Loughlins of Ballyvaughan in County Clare as the result of a stolen cow having been brought to their town, and of the consequent payments and fines in which this involved them.

The County Kilkenny reference of 1537 quoted above shows the 'whole kindred' of both the murdered man and the murderer as the active parties in the ensuing litigation. This was one of the most basic principles of the Irish legal system, the law of *cin comhfhocuis*, anglicised as Kincogish, by which the corporate family was responsible for the acts of each of its members. This rule was early adopted by English law in its dealings with the Irishry; it is mentioned in an early statute of 1278, and is enshrined as a principle in several statutes of the fifteenth and sixteenth centuries. Although the adoption of the principle into English law was disapproved of by many administrators and observers of the Elizabethan period, it was apparently regarded as impossible to administer the Irish territories without its use. But the principle of joint responsibility was carried further than the actual kindred, and could affect communities as well. The famous Statute of Kilkenny in 1366 forbade, by one of its clauses, the practice of holding Irishmen and their goods responsible for the debts incurred by their local lord or chief, unless they had actually become surety for the latter. It would be a natural principle that if the immediate kindred failed in their responsibility, the latter should be extended to a wider group. The great *eric* of 340 cows which the earl of Kildare exacted in 1554 for the slaying of his foster-brother by one of the Mac Coghlans was assessed upon the whole territory of Delvin-Mac Coghlan, but it is to be noted that one of the three rival and hostile septs into which the Mac Coghlans were divided refused to pay the third assessed on them, no doubt feeling that only the actual kindred of the slayer – who belonged to one of the other septs – should contribute.

The law of land; 'Irish gavelkind'

The customs of land-tenure and ownership in Ireland must have varied, not only between one area and another, but also often between one clan and another within the same area, for it is obvious that an arrangement which had been followed by a particular family over some generations would come to have the force of custom and thus of law. It must of course be remembered that the account given here is concerned only with the land-titles of the dominant class; the weight of evidence is strongly against the existence of any system of peasant-right in the actual cultivators. One must beware, however, of ascribing an excessive rigidity or even consistency to the details of medieval Irish land-holding; just as in the period of the last Carolingians in France a grant of land made by a king for two lives only would have converted itself in the second generation into a perpetual allodial ownership, so in Ireland in the marcher areas a grant of land to hold at will, if allowed to continue over several generations, was felt to establish a definite freehold interest in the heirs of the grantee. Again, the process of encroachment by the expanding ruling clans on the lesser land-owning clans in possession seems sometimes to have created a double layer of land-titles, in which the older group, although reduced to holding their lands as 'tenants-at-will', would continue to claim a title to it. We have no detailed account of the building up of any group of clan lands in the medieval period, but the process is unlikely to have differed much – save, perhaps, in the greater employment of mere force – from that by which at a later date such a man as Tibbot *na long* Bourke, first Viscount Mayo (died 1629), built up his enormous estates – pledge and purchase from his own poorer clansmen and from the members of neighbouring declining clans. The methods and pressures by which the chiefs and their immediate kin were able to build up their property at the expense of the weaker landowners have been already alluded to (Chapter II). It is probable that in many cases lands which were still in the possession of the original proprietors were included in the partitions made between members of chiefly clans. In the territory of Pobal Caoch in County Galway, which took its name from Teig Caoch O Kelly (died 1484) and was divided among his descendants, much of the land still belonged in the sixteenth and early seventeenth centuries to the family of Mac Ward, who had been there long before the time of Teig Caoch. Everywhere, also, a vast amount of the land must have been actually held under ancient pledges which could be expected never to be, and in fact would never be, redeemed, while such customs as that referred to above (Chapter II), by which a chief would have custody of the lands of an absent landowner, and that referred to as being 'the use and custom in the Irish countries of the county of Galway, and in most of the other countries and territories of the mere Irishry', which allowed neighbouring and related clans to occupy for grazing lands which were lying waste owing to the 'absence and decay' of the clan to which they belonged, must have led to many conflicts and confusion regarding proprietorship.

The word gavelkind was of course an English term originally denoting the custom of inheritance which prevailed in Kent – where alone in England the rule of partition between sons instead of primogeniture survived the twelfth century – and borrowed by sixteenth-century writers to denote the system of inheritance which existed in Wales and Ireland, by which lands were 'parted and partible amongst the issue male of any dying possessed thereof'. The formal legal phrase was 'custom in nature of gavelkind'. Although the rule of primogeniture may have seemed the norm to later English observers, it was far from being the universal or even general practice of Europe; the system of partition which prevailed in the middle ages and after among the princely houses of Germany is well known, and at a lower level of society partible inheritance was almost everywhere the norm outside England. The system of partible inheritance, under which all sons shared equally, which we find in the fifteenth and sixteenth centuries in force in such Anglo-Irish towns as Galway and Athenry – and probably the others as well – may have owed more to old rules of borough inheritance and to the influence of the Roman law than it did to 'Irish gavelkind'. What was the peculiar feature of the latter system was that the unit of proprietorship was not the individual as such but the family group viewed as a corporation (see Chapter I) and the consequent fact that the holdings of the various members of the group were liable to redistribution from time to time (see below). This shifting of shares was a strong disincentive to the holder to erect permanent buildings or otherwise improve his holding (just as was tenancy-at-will at a lower social and economic level, in sixteenth- and nineteenth-century Ireland alike) and was to afford powerful ammunition to English critics of the custom. Other features of the system strange to English eyes but shared by Welsh and Irish law were that the illegitimate – even 'named' or affiliated sons (see Chapter IV) – were admitted to shares along with the legitimate, and that women were entirely excluded from inheritance.

The exclusion of women was a natural consequence of the concept of the family corporation as the landowning unit, as a woman's children would of course belong to their fathers' clans, not to their mother's, and so would have no claim to share in the inheritance of the latter. The principle was early adopted, as is well known, by the descendants of the Anglo-Norman settlers in Ireland. In Elizabethan times the Irish Court of Chancery, although ready to enforce the rule of 'gavelkind' inheritance, refused to accept this exclusion of women and ordered that daughters should inherit in the absence of sons. The defendant in a Chancery suit of 1595, speaking of the Irish and Gaelicised Norman territories of County Westmeath, says that 'as to the custom that a woman should not inherit . . . the same is against law and reason . . . and by several decrees in this honourable Court the said custom hath been disallowed.' Ten years later another Chancery pleading says that in Ormond 'by the general wrongful usurpation of that country they do not willingly permit any woman to inherit her ancestors' inheritance.' Although a woman could not inherit the lands of her clan she was, of course, perfectly free to acquire land by pledge or purchase, and it was in fact normal for women to receive lands in pledge for their dowries, either from their fathers or kinsfolk or from their husbands. Furthermore, as it seems to have been the general rule in all parts of Ireland that a man could freely bequeath lands that he had purchased or acquired in pledge – as these would not form part of the corporate clan property – there would seem to have been no restriction on his bequeathing such acquisitions to a daughter or sister.

Forms of partition

The particular forms of division in 'Irish gavelkind' and the occasions of redistribution within the clan varied considerably in different areas. Sir John Davys says 'after partition made, if any one of the sept died, his portion was not divided among his sons, but the chief of the sept made a new partition of all the lands belonging to that sept and gave to every one his part according to his antiquity [seniority].' This is almost precisely what we find in surviving Chancery pleadings of the 1590s relating to the Westmeath-Offaly area, but here the actual partition was not made by the chief but by the most junior of the coheirs entitled to share – who, as having to receive the share left over after all his seniors had chosen theirs, would have had the strongest incentive to make the fairest and most equal division possible – and the coheirs then chose their shares in order of seniority. On the death of any of the coheirs, a fresh division took place, the seniors again taking first choice. In Thomond and some other parts of northern Munster there is some evidence that the sons of a deceased elder brother were given the preferential choice over their seniors by birth. Although in these areas a fresh division only took place on the death of a coheir, in other areas it was the rule to make a new division every year. In 1550 it is said that among the O Connors of Offaly it was the custom that the eldest of each clan could redistribute the lands at his will among the members every Mayday and take, as the senior, the best portion for himself. This power of the chief to make the actual division was certainly, in spite of Davy's statement, far from universal; it seems, however, to have been prevalent in Munster, where an inquisition of 1594 states that the chief of the O Callaghans in County Cork could redistribute the lands of the ruling sept – which amounted to the greater part of the O Callaghan territory – at his will amongst his kinsmen who held them. Such a power vested in the chiefs must have immensely strengthened their position towards their clansmen, and in it we may find the explanation of why the Munster chiefs were so often in possession of such disproportionately large parts of their clan territories.

In Connacht the practice of making a new division among the clan every Mayday was probably general; as late as 1624 the lands of the O Kellys of Kyleawoga, comprising a large group of townlands, were still being divided amongst the members of the sept – whose relationship to each other was that of second cousins – 'but from Mayday to Mayday during pleasure'. It is significant that although the shares of these coheirs, expressed as fractions of each of the various townlands of the estate, had been surrendered to the Crown and individually regranted in the general surrender and regrant of Connacht in 1618, the practice of annual redistribution continued, and a comparison of the holdings of Connacht landowners in 1618 with those in 1638 shows that in many cases redistribution within the clans, quite apart from actual changes of proprietorship, must have taken place in the meantime. It would seem that the minute fractions of the various townlands of an estate – and also of castles – which we find assigned to individual proprietors in Connacht and elsewhere in sixteenth- and seventeenth-century records represent neither individually divided shares nor shares in the rent of the townland as a whole, but shares in the ultimate legal proprietorship of the whole estate. This in fact would have been divided into temporary shares, no doubt conveniently set out in a single location but redistributed at intervals, between the various coheirs. When we find two brothers of the O Byrnes holding a hundred and twelfth part of twenty-six townlands, scattered over a distance of nearly thirty miles in County Wicklow, it is obvious that their interest did not consist of shares in each townland but of shares in the group as a whole.

After two or three generations the corporate clan would normally have been too extended and too riven by internal dissension to function effectively, and in such cases a permanent division of its land would have been made between its members. Some documents relating to such permanent divisions still survive and throw further light on the system. An award of 1587 shows a younger brother refusing to leave the lands which he had occupied all his life in favour of his elder brother, who had chosen them by his right of first choice in the partition which had been made. By the award the occupier was left in possession, on paying compensation to his senior. An interesting document, formerly in the Public Record Office of Ireland, recorded the proceedings in 1584 between the members of a clan of the O Kennedys in Ormond over the question as to whether in fact a permanent division had been previously made or not. One branch of the clan, whose share of the lands was in other townlands, claimed a share also in the castle of Ballycapple, the chief place of the clan. The branch who were actually in possession maintained that a permanent division had been made long before and that under it they had held Bally-capple for eighty years without dispute. This the claimants countered by the argument that the eighty years' possession, which they admitted, had been simply owing to the defendants' relative seniority within the clan (the defen-dants were a grandson and great-grandson of the clan founder, while the claimants were great-great-grandsons). The arbitrators awarded that the existing division should remain in force, except as regards the castle and its bawns, which were to be held by the senior of the clan for the time being, to whichever branch he might belong. Any other member of the clan was to have the right to build a house within the bawn, on paying certain rents in food and rendering certain labour services to the senior. To show the complications which could arise under 'Irish gavelkind' tenure, the complainants in this case were shortly afterwards sued for half their lands by a local notable who claimed by a conveyance from an alleged cousin of theirs whose relationship they denied, main-taining that his alleged grandfather – their granduncle – had in fact died sonless.

It will be easily seen from the important place occupied

in the system by the senior (*sinnsear*) or clan head (*ceannfine*) why it was normal for English writers to link 'gavelkind' with 'tanistry', that is, with the principle of succession by seniority. In the case of small clan holdings it would seem that often – especially, perhaps, in Munster, the senior of the clan was the actual possessor of all its land. A pleading of one Teige O Molawn in County Cork in 1596 states that it was the custom in the lands of the clan, called Ferran O Molawn, that on the death of any person possessed of lands his lands should pass to 'the next eldest, best and most worthy' of the clan. The exact position of the *ceannfine* with regard to his kinsmen must, however, have varied not only between area and area but between one individual clan and another.

Customs approaching 'gavelkind'

The system of equal division among sons described above prevailed not only among clans of purely Gaelic origin but among the completely Gaelicised Anglo-Norman ones – those of Connacht and of the Westmeath border – Dillons, Daltons and Delamares. In Munster the Burkes of Clanwilliam in Counties Limerick and Tipperary and the Barrets of County Cork seem also to have followed it. Throughout most of the Anglo-Norman lordships of Munster, however, and in some other marcher areas we find an intermediate system by which, although the estate was not liable to equal division among the males of the family, the younger sons were nevertheless entitled to a share of the land. In 1558 it is said to be a custom used time out of mind by the Powers in County Waterford that 'the second brethren should have of their fathers' inheritance certain portion of land assigned and allotted unto them' and the same custom is also specifically referred to among the Barrys of County Cork, while the evidence to be deduced from land-ownership patterns shows that it must have been general in the Norman areas of Munster where equal division was not in practice. The same would apply to other marcher areas. In 1501 we find a Nicholas Nugent of Westmeath directing in a testamentary deed that his two sons should be entirely equal in their inheritance of his lands, and this Nicholas was himself an illegitimate son to whom his father and legitimate brother had granted portions of the family lands.

The pledge of land

The usual method by which land would change hands both in Gaelic Ireland and in the marcher areas was the pledge, or 'mortgage' as it is called in sixteenth and seventeenth-century English documents, although, as the pledgee took actual possession of the land and held it until it was redeemed from him, the term 'mortgage' is technically incorrect. In its simplest form the pledge was an arrangement by which A advanced a sum in money or cattle to B, receiving in return a piece of land which he occupied until the sum was repaid, but all sorts of debts and charges could be and were converted into pledges on land. We have already seen how lords and chiefs would convert their unpaid exactions and coyne and livery into pledges on the land on which they had been levied. An Irish document of 1556 from County Clare shows us how various debts would be converted into pledges. Donnell Óg O Kearney had originally been tenant of Ballymote to Sheeda Mac Namara, and certain horses of his had been seized by O Brien's stewards for the tributes which Mac Namara owed. An award laid down that O Kearney should have their value as a pledge on Ballymote. After Sheeda's death some followers of his heir, Donnell Derg, stole two pigs from O Kearney, and the consequent damages were added to the amount of the pledge. When Donnell Derg was arrested for debt in the city of Limerick, O Kearney paid the debt and released him, and when he was subsequently held as a prisoner for his unpaid gambling debts and redeemed by another Mac Namara, O Kearney paid the latter all or part of what it had cost him, likewise receiving this sum as a pledge on Ballymote. He had also advanced a sum of money to Donnell Derg on the security of the same lands. An important feature of the system was that the pledgee in possession would continue to advance further sums of money or cattle to the pledger on the security of the same land. Sometimes this was expressly provided for in the original agreement – thus a deed of pledge of 1535 from County Kilkenny lays down that if the pledgers should afterwards 'to their need' desire any further advances on the land then the pledgee will advance as much as two impartial arbitrators will award. This system of further advances worked to the benefit of both parties; the pledger secured an advance on the security of land which was not in his possession and from which he was deriving no actual benefit, while the pledgee, by increasing the amount of the pledge, diminished the possibility of the land being redeemed. Eventually, as was the case of certain lands in Ormond in 1578, the lands might be in pledge 'for so large a number of cows that it would be difficult for any to redeem them'. In such a case, or if the heirs of the original pledger had become extinct or had forgotten their rights through sinking into poverty or emigrating from the district, the land would remain in the undisturbed possession of the heirs of the pledgee. The interest of the pledgee in possession and the right of redemption in the pledger and his heirs would each of course descend according to the normal rules of Irish succession by 'gavelkind'.

The provisions for the redemption of the land pledged were often very complicated and hedged about with restrictions for the benefit of the pledgee. Commonly the pledge could not be redeemed before a certain number of years had elapsed, and a common proviso, especially in marcher areas, was that the pledgee might retain possession of the lands at a specified low rent for a specified number of years after he had been repaid in full. Redemption had normally to be made at Mayday or at Michaelmas, or within a short period after one of these terms, and a County Wexford mortgage of the 1590s laid down that the sum might be repaid only between 8 and 12 a.m. on Mayday, and that the offer of repayment must be 'at the gate' of the land in question. The terms of the pledge might lay down that the pledgee was entitled to compensation for any buildings he might erect on the land, but it would seem that in any case he was entitled to demand this. A very common condition was that the land could only be redeemed by the pledger or his heirs with their own goods or money – thus preventing them from assigning the pledge to a third party.

4 Social Life and Groups

The people

It has been suggested that the population of late medieval Ireland was divided into two sharply opposed classes, the 'free' – consisting of the landowners and some other privileged groups – and the 'unfree', but this seems a mistaken deduction from the statements of sixteenth-century English writers regarding the position of the peasantry vis-à-vis their lords. Fynes Moryson, for instance, says that the 'lords challenged right of inheritance in their tenants' persons, as if by old covenants they were born slaves to till their ground and to do them all services and howsoever they were oppressed might not leave their lord to dwell under any other landlord. And suits between the lords for right in tenants were then most frequent.' In 1585 the Irish Privy Council commanded that the tenants of the earl of Clancare, 'who had lately departed from him, contrary to the custom of the country', should be forced to return to him. Certainly, at the close of the sixteenth century, the lords claimed a right to retain their tenants and denied the latters' right to leave. But this does not, I think, entitle us to regard Irish society as being divided into a free and a servile class. If it had been, one would expect to find some mention of these serfs in some of the surviving legal documents, and yet there is none. In a document of 1547 concerning the lordship of Kerrycurrihy in County Cork, it is true, there would appear to be mention of such a class, referred to as 'bondmen and villains'. The document tells us that Sir Thomas of Desmond (afterwards earl) and Cormac Óg Mac Carthy, lord of Muskerry, had imposed coyne and livery on certain lands in spite of the fact that the latter, being held of the bishop of Cork, were traditionally free from all such impositions, because the tenants of the lands in question happened to be their 'bondmen', claiming the right to tax 'their own bondmen and servants where they might find them'. The document, however, speaks of one of the persons in question, a 'bondman and servant' of Sir Thomas of Desmond called Donnell O Mahony, as 'a great gentleman of the said lands' – a strange description for a 'bondman and villain' – and it seems clear from certain statements in the document that these 'bondmen' were in fact the 'middlemen' – to use the nineteenth-century term – of the lands between the proprietors and the actual cultivators, the 'poor tenants' as they are called in the document. We are thus dealing with persons of fairly high social and economic status, and it seems to me that by the term 'bondmen' is to be understood nothing more than that the persons in question were subjects of the lords – of their *oireacht* – born within the territories ruled by the latter, and that it corresponds in meaning with the 'followers' of a slightly later date.

I think that the rights claimed by sixteenth-century Irish lords over their tenants – and it is largely on the existence of these rights that the argument for the division of society into a free and an unfree class rests – represent as described a confusion of two different elements: firstly, the rights which the lord of a country claimed over his subjects, those dwelling within it, and secondly, a right of the landlord to retain his tenant which was primarily of contractual origin. We have seen how Moryson refers to 'old covenants', and it is possible that the acceptance by a peasant of land or stock from a landowner was held to bind him thereafter to the latter and his heirs. In a country where the hereditary principle was of such strength as it was in Ireland, it is easy to understand how in its final development such a contractual relationship might be claimed as binding on the descendants of the original party. But the proclamation of 1605 which abolished all such rights, by declaring in its operative clause that such 'unfree' persons were henceforth 'not to be called the natives or natural followers of any . . lord or chieftain whatsoever' suggests, as does the Kerrycurrihy document of 1547 already quoted, that what was being referred to was basically a political right based on the rule of an area.

That the distinction, however, which has been drawn between the 'free' and 'unfree' elements of the population is certainly unreal in legal terms must not blind us to its reality in social and economic ones. In practice the status of the great mass of the population in Gaelic Ireland, the actual cultivators and labourers – 'churls', as they are referred to by contemporary English writers – was very low indeed. Economic factors alone are sufficient explanation of this, without the need to postulate any hereditary condition of unfreedom. Indeed the poorer landowners, their lands divided by 'Irish gavelkind' into ever smaller shares which, under the pressure of their lords' exactions as well as of sheer economic necessity they would be forced to pledge or otherwise alienate without any hope of redemption, must have been constantly slipping into the ranks of the depressed classes. Their actual position would have been much inferior to that of the members of such rising and influential, although landless, clans as the O Harts of Sligo or the O Riordans and Clancallaghans in Muskerry, who lived as tenants on the extensive demesne lands of some lord or powerful clan. These landless clans of 'followers', who nevertheless were people of consequence, are to be found especially in Munster. They seem, as one would expect, to have flourished only when large tracts of land remained in the hands of a single lord or a small kinship group.

Without any stake in the land such as that given by the peasant-right – the right to occupy and cultivate the land on paying the lord's dues – of feudally organised countries, the Irish cultivator was in a particularly weak economic position. His actual condition would have principally depended on whether or not he possessed any stock of his own; if he did, his position might be tolerable and he might even acquire land on pledge from some depressed landowner, and become a person of some standing in society. The *Annals of Ulster* record once or twice the death of a person described as *scológ maith*, the literal translation of which term would be 'a well-to-do farmer'. Without stock of his own, the cultivator would be little better than a sharecropping labourer, totally dependent on the master he followed. That the peasantry did not bear arms was simply a consequence of their function and economic position, and the fact that Shane O Neill, as Sir Henry Sidney tells us in a much-quoted passage, was the first Irishman that armed the peasantry of his country can and should be seen, not as a defiance of an established social custom, but as an indication of the growing disorder and the breakdown of economic life in a country given over increasingly to war.

There is no material available which would enable us to give an estimate of Irish population, even in any particular area, during the late medieval period. That it was low even by contemporary standards is suggested by the very low value of land shown in contemporary deeds of sale and mortgage.

Nomenclature

Some words may be said on the forms of Irish personal nomenclature in the medieval period, as these frequently cause confusion to those unacquainted with the subject.

The use of the patronymic in addition to, or instead of, a surname was almost universal in Gaelic and Gaelicised Ireland and in the Irish towns, being rare or absent only in the city of Dublin and in the Pale. The use of a double or even triple patronymic is common, and indeed one cannot theoretically draw a line of distinction between an individual's patronymic – *qua* 'name' – and the genealogical recitation of his descent, the patronymic being in essence a short genealogy attached to the individual's name. The patronymic was formed in Irish with *mac*, in English with *fitz*, prefixed to the father's name; during the fifteenth and early sixteenth centuries, forms with suffixed *-son* (as Richard Shaneson, Gerrot Jamesson) occur in Anglo-Norman areas, but they seem to have later died out. When the son's name was identical with that of the father, it was more usual, instead of, or as well as the patronymic, to add the adjective oge (*óg*, young) to the son's name and in the case of three generations of the same name we find such forms as Shane esogy (*is óige*, 'the youngest') or Cormac Óg Beg (*beag*, 'little'). It must be remembered that a patronymic in mac or fitz, as found in contemporary documents, is a living recitation and not a fixed name, and that when, for instance, we find a reference to 'Rosse mcCoyne son to Brian O Connor' it was of course not Rosse but his father Conn (Coyne represents the Irish genitive form, *Cuinn*) who was Brian's son. The patronymic may either precede or follow the surname, but more difficulty is created by the common use of the patronymic without a surname at all. This is most usual in the case of great stocks such as the Geraldines, but occurs frequently in all classes of society. It was more common in the south than in the north of Ireland. The feminine equivalent of both O and *Mac* was *inghean*, 'daughter', shortened in current usage into *ní* or *'nín* (nyne).

Closely allied to the use of patronymics was that of

nicknames or epithets attached to the name. These reflected some personal characteristic, colour of hair, a defect such as lameness (as in the case of Conn *Bacach* O Neill, Con the lame) or bad sight, etc., in which case they were often highly insulting, though accepted without question by the individuals to whom they were applied. One must note, however, that such epithets might be applied ironically, expressing the opposite of a person's real characteristics – or they might sometimes be derived from a place where the individual in question had been fostered or had spent some time. Like a patronymic, a nickname might be used to the exclusion of the surname.

Marriage and sexual life

In no field of life was Ireland's apartness from the mainstream of Christian European society so marked as in that of marriage. Throughout the medieval period, and down to the end of the old order in 1603, what could be called Celtic secular marriage remained the norm in Ireland and Christian matrimony was no more than the rare exception grafted on to this system. Sir John Popham, attorney-general, writing in 1587 of the Munster gentry, declared that no more than one in twenty was married in church, but this may be an exaggeration. This secular marriage permitted easy divorce, and it was normal in late medieval Ireland for men and women of the upper classes to have a succession of spouses. Dubhchabhlaigh Mór ('the great', as she was called), who died in 1395 and who was a daughter of Cathal O Connor, King of Connacht, was nicknamed *Port-na-dtrí-namhad* ('the meeting-place of the three enemies') because she was married to three lords who were sworn enemies to each other, as well as to other men. Ulick *na gceann* de Burgo, first earl of Clanrickard, was survived by two wives, each of whom claimed to have been his legitimate wife and her son the heir. The question was eventually decided in favour of Grany ny Carroll, her alleged previous marriage to another man being declared invalid. Her son, the second earl of Clanrickard, Ricard 'Sassanach', was six times married; a list of his wives, probably drawn up not long before his death in 1582, tells us that five of them were then living, four (including his first wife, the mother of the third earl) having been put away by him in turn. In a lawsuit of 1624, the defendants, in impugning the legitimacy of the plaintiff's father, declare that at the date of his parent's marriage each of them had two previous spouses, whom they had married 'in face of Holy Church', still living. Such an *ex parte* statement may well in this instance be untrue, but it reflects a state of things which other evidence shows to have been common.

The canon law of the medieval Church, preserved until modern times in the marriage law of Scotland, insisted that no outward ceremony was necessary for a valid marriage, and that the mere declaration, or even intent, of the parties, followed by consummation, constituted a permanently valid and binding, although clandestine, marriage. This would seem to have made Irish secular marriages into valid marriages in the eyes of the Church, but there was one fatal flaw. In order to allow a valid marriage, there must be no existing impediment. The medieval Church forbade marriage, except by papal dispensation, between all those related up to the degree of third cousins. After the thirteenth century this was extended to cover those related by affinity as well, that is by a previous relationship by marriage or sexual intercourse with a person related to the other party within the forbidden degrees of relationship. The Irish in practice usually married their kinsfolk, while their promiscuity created innumerable ties by 'affinity', so that most of their marriages were invalid in canon law. Only the richest would or could go to the expense and trouble of obtaining a dispensation – and indeed it was not until after 1400 that dispensations for marriage began to be given as a matter of course. In any case, given the climate of sexual freedom which existed, it seems to have been more usual – in Ireland as in Scotland – to enter into a trial marriage *before* obtaining the dispensation. The majority, perhaps, of Irish marriage dispensations recorded in the papal registers declare that the parties have already cohabited and had children. The same source shows that the greater number of Irish clerics – who presumably in this were representative of the population as a whole – were the children of parents related within the canonically forbidden degrees. The difficulties created by the canon law prohibition of marriage within such wide degrees of relationship or affinity were experienced in every European country in the later middle ages. But in Ireland, where the Church seems to have had no practical success in enforcing its prohibition of the marriage of kinsfolk, their effects must have been more noticeable than elsewhere and must have been a most important factor in ensuring the continuance of the native law of marriage.

There is little information regarding marriages between kinsfolk nearer than first cousins. We know that Turlough O Connor, king of Connacht (died 1340), divorced his first wife in order to marry his own maternal aunt, Sir Edmund de Burgo's widow, and the relationship between James, third earl of Ormond and his niece (sister's daughter), Katherine of Desmond, was probably not unique. The story, as told in a seventeenth-century genealogical collection, is highly scandalous (she left her father's home after being caught in an affair with her brother, was raped by her uncle Ormond with whom she had taken refuge, and thereafter regularised her position by poisoning his English countess, etc.) but much of this may be later imagination; that it should have been told in this form is however highly significant. From documentary evidence we know that the earl sought, apparently unsuccessfully, for a papal dispensation to marry her, in default of which he made an enormous settlement upon her and her sons by him, the ancestors of the later Butlers of Cahir. Sir George Carew, in his collection of genealogies of the Munster nobility, names two individuals born of brother-sister relationships – one involving the Sugaun Earl of Desmond – and one of father-daughter incest (the father in this case being the last White Knight, the famous Edmond). Such examples are unlikely to have been common, but it must be remembered that the custom of fosterage, which reduced normal family contact, and the general climate of sexual permissiveness would probably have made them less unlikely to happen in Ireland than elsewhere.

In early times it was the custom for the husband to make a marriage-gift (*coibhche* or *tionnscra*) to the bride, and two fourteenth-century bishops of Raphoe are recorded to have pledged lands which belonged to the see to their wives for this purpose, but the custom would seem to have become obsolete by the sixteenth century. By the same period, and probably under the influence of Roman law, the stock (*spréidh*) which the woman had been accustomed to receive from her own family on setting up home seems to have been converted into a dowry paid to the husband, although he still remained liable for its repayment in case of divorce. Some late sixteenth-century depositions regarding the marriage of a great County Waterford lord, Mac Thomas (his name was Thomas fitz Richard, and he was head of a collateral branch of the Desmond Geraldines) to one Margaret Tobin, show us the bride's parents seeking contributions among their kinsfolk towards the amount of the 'marriage goods' or dowry, which in this case amounted to 80 cows, 24 stud mares, 5 riding horses, a pair of chessboards and a harp, with household utensils. This, from other examples, would seem to have been an average amount among the upper classes. The dowries of lesser folk would seem to have always included such essential domestic furniture as a pot and a gridiron. Mac Thomas afterwards put Margaret Tobin away 'without divorce, aid or consent of Holy Church' and took another wife, without repaying any of the dowry, and the Tobins in consequence sued Lord Power, who had become surety for its repayment in such circumstances. It was customary to insist upon sureties for the repayment of the dowry in case of divorce or the husband's death; in the latter case the wife by Irish law would have no claim to the husband's lands, unless they had been specifically pledged for this purpose. In a marriage treaty in Irish from County Clare, of 1560, the bridegroom not only gives sureties for repayment but also pledges certain lands for that purpose.

Affiliation; the 'naming' of children
It has been mentioned that the Irish law did not distinguish in matters of succession between the legitimate and the illegitimate, all being equally entitled to share in the paternal estate. This applied not only to the children of temporary marriages such as those referred to above and to the offspring of recognised concubines, but also to those born of casual relationships and afterwards affiliated by the sworn declaration of their mothers. This was the well-known custom of the 'naming' of children, described by Fynes Moryson as

> a ridiculous custom that married women give fathers to their children when they are on the point of death . . . commonly they give them fathers of the O Neills, O Donnells or such great men . . . And these bastard children ever after follow these fathers and, thinking themselves to descend from them, will be called swordsmen and, scorning husbandry and manual arts, live only of rapine and spoil.

References to the practice are numerous in contemporary records. The most famous example, of course, is that of Matthew or Feardoragh O Neill, baron of Dungannon and the father of Hugh, earl of Tyrone, whose mother was the wife of a smith in Dundalk and who, according to the account, admittedly prejudiced, of Shane O Neill, until he reached

> the age of 15 or 16 years was taken and named none other than Matthew Kelly, and no man knew him to be otherwise than the smith of Dundalk's son, born in wedlock, till a little after that age his mother, for vainglory and for a name for herself, declared him to be O Neill's son, alleging and boasting how O Neill lay once with her. And O Neill [Conn Bacach, first earl of Tyrone] being a man that never refused no child that any woman named to be his, as he had divers besides the said Matthew, accepted and took him to be his son.

But there are other examples of persons who changed paternity even later in life. Hugh O Gallagher, afterwards O Donnell, 'was for many years supposed and taken to be son to Dean O Gallagher' and married a daughter of Calvagh O Donnell; in middle age he changed paternity and was accepted as a son of the late Calvagh. James Meagh, until he was 40 years old, was reputed to have been the son of William Meagh (died 1548), the Henrician bishop of Kildare. He was then 'named' as son to the long-deceased Kedagh O More and was actually elected as chief of the O Mores; in his will, made in 1584, he styles himself, as he is styled in contemporary documents, 'James Meagh *alias* James mac Kedagh O More'. In 1400 a Connacht cleric, James de Bermingham, was dispensed for illegitimacy and provided to a benefice by the pope, 'notwithstanding that he has been transferred from one putative father to another father'. The custom was forbidden by the provincial synod of Cashel held at Limerick in 1453, which declared that the mother was not to be believed if she transferred her children from one father to another, and this prohibition, repeated by another provincial synod there in 1502, was probably laid down by ecclesiastical councils elsewhere as well. In view of the perseverance of the custom, it would seem to have had little, if any, effect.

Fosterage

The custom of fosterage, by which persons of importance would commit the upbringing of their children to others, is well known. The practice was of considerable political importance, for the person so fostered could count on the adherence of his foster-family throughout life; thus the great Shane O Neill, having been fostered by the O Donnellys (whence his epithet of Shane *Donnghaileach*), the hereditary marshals to the O Neills, enjoyed their support throughout his career. Conversely, the fosterers would also reap the benefits of support and protection, and Campion declares – probably with some exaggeration – that 'commonly 500 kine and more are given to win a nobleman's child to foster'. When Thomas, earl of Ormond, entered into a treaty with O Mulrian and his brother in 1557 one of the conditions was that he should give them the first son or daughter to be born to him in fosterage. Even the clergy habitually took children to foster; Patrick O Sgannell, a Dominican friar who was successively bishop of Raphoe and primate of Armagh, fostered a daughter of Godfrey O Donnell, king of Tirconnell. The synod of Limerick in 1453 forbade the clergy to take noblemen's children in fosterage without episcopal licence.

The professional learned classes

A distinctive element in medieval Irish society was

constituted by the families who followed as hereditary occupations the various learned professions; the hereditary jurists – who have been already referred to in Chapter III, the scholars and historians, the hereditary physicians, the harpers and – most distinctive of all – the poets. Like the clergy, with whom they shared the common bond of literacy and with whom they – except perhaps to some degree the poets, whose tradition was more deeply rooted in paganism – were closely connected, the professional learned men were exempted from such secular burdens as military service in the *gairmsluaigh* or 'rising-out' of the country (see below) and they often held lands free of tribute and exactions in return for exercising their professions. Their connection with the church is manifested by the number of learned families who were erenaghs upon church lands; in Fermanagh the O Breslin jurists, the historian O Cianains and O Luinins, the physician O Cassidys and the poetic O Fialains all were erenaghs, while another poetic family of the area, the O Husseys, were probably also of ecclesiastical origin. While these families were usually associated with a single profession – this was especially characteristic of the jurists and the physicians – some exercised more than one; the Magraths of Munster were both poets and historians from an early date, while the O Duigenans seem to have combined the profession of history with that of music, and all the historian families turned their hand on occasion to the poetic craft. Most of these learned families first appear in history in the thirteenth century, but to this the poets are an exception; the Munster poetic families of Magrath and O Quill can both be traced back to the eleventh century, while the O Dalys and O Donnellans in Meath and Connacht respectively, appear in the twelfth, and it is possible that some of the poetic families had in fact exercised their craft since pagan times. Some of the physician families must also have been of early origin, as is shown by such of their surnames as O Hicky (from *Icidhe*, 'healer') and Mac Inlea (*liaigh*, 'leech'), although they – unless indeed they possessed an oral tradition quite distinct from their written one – do not seem to have preserved any native medical lore; the texts which they studied and copied were the usual stock-in-trade of contemporary European medicine, such as the *Aphorisms of Hippocrates*, the *Rosa Anglica* of John of Gaddesden and the writings of Bernard of Gordon. The musicians, who by the nature of their profession left no literary remains, are for this reason the least-known of the professional groups. The musicians were, for obvious reasons, among the first of the Gaelic learned men to be patronised by the Anglo-Normans; when John de Bermingham, earl of Louth, and his followers were massacred by the English gentry of Louth in 1329 there fell in his company Mulroony Mac Carroll, the most distinguished musician of his day, with his brother and twenty of his pupils.

The title of ollave (*ollamh*) was given to the officially recognised head of one of the learned professions within a particular territory, appointed by and serving the lord of the territory and styled indifferently ollave of the territory in question or of its ruler. The official brehon, already referred to, was ollave in law within his territory, and there might be similar ollaves in history, medicine, poetry or music. In 1473 James, lord Courcy of Kinsale granted to one Rory Mac Betha, physician, certain lands along with 'medical dignity and liberty throughout my lordship'. This Rory, who thus turns up in County Cork, belonged to a family whose headquarters were in the western Isles of Scotland, illustrating another feature of the learned families, their 'cosmopolitanism' within the Gaelic world. A century later O Connor physicians, whose native place was on the flanks of Slieve Bloom in County Laois, turn up in the Highlands. Such wanderings would not only be for the purpose of exercising their professions but also, and more especially, for study; many of the professional families kept schools at which their arts were taught, and we find members of these families at study in places far removed from their homes.

The poets

The poets (*aos dána; fileadha*, sing. *file*) were the most striking group of the professional learned classes. The poet, it must first be emphasised, was much more than a mere composer of verse, and his position in late medieval Irish society represented a most extraordinary survival from an earlier and pre-Christian phase of Celtic life. For the poet was a sacred personage, almost a priest or magician. His versified curses (usually miscalled 'satires' in English, but their purpose was magical harm, not ridicule) could injure and kill those against whom they were directed. Niall O Higgin, a member of one of the greatest poetic families who lived at the commencement of the fifteenth century, is credited with two such 'poet's miracles' against those who had plundered him; the second of these being no less than the death of Sir John Stanley, Lord Lieutenant of Ireland, who died from the effects of O Higgin's curses five weeks after he had plundered the poet. In 1495 Cian O Gara, a gentleman of County Sligo, is recorded to have died of a similar miracle. The sacred character of the poet led to his enjoying a status of immunity equal to, if not exceeding, that of the church, while his powers of cursing were placed in strange juxta-position to the church's power of excommunication, both being invoked against the violators of treaties of which 'the Holy Church and the rhymers', wielders of the twin powers of curse, Christian and pagan respectively, were invoked as sureties (above, Chapter III).

'Rhymers' is the normal term for the poets in con-temporary English sources. The term bard, now in general use, seems even in the sixteenth century to have denoted, as it did in earlier times, an inferior class of poet. A list of the 'poets, chroniclers and rhymers' in County Cork, drawn up in 1584, seems to distinguish between 'rhymers' and 'bards' and shows that O Daly Finn, the chief poet (*ollamh dána*, ollave in poetry) of Desmond, had his bard. The well-known account of the poets by the contemporary Thomas Smyth also refers to the poet being accompanied by his attendant bard, who was no doubt a less-qualified person who acted as an assistant. The list of 1584 also notes the existence of woman bards. The basic profession of the poet, from which he earned his living, was of course the eulogy of the great and the glorification of their deeds, and it was this function of the poets as the panegyrists of the old order, the praisers and inciters of violence and spoil, which are dwelt on with such emphasis by Smyth and which earned them the bitter hostility of the government in the period of the reconquest. A series of sixteenth-century enactments classed the poets with rogues and vagabonds and proscribed them accordingly. Some of the order may have fallen victim to these enactments, but the more important members of the great poetic clans, secure in their wealth and in their often considerable landed possessions, would have had little to fear from them. Smyth gives a graphic description of the poet inciting his youthful patron to a *creach* (cattle-raid) and being rewarded out of the spoil; he furnishes us with interesting details which would otherwise remain unknown to us, such as the fact that the praise-poem, when completed, was delivered not by the poet himself – who could hardly be expected always to possess a good voice as well as his professional talents – but by a professional reciter (*reacaire*), while a harper provided an accompaniment.

A curious perquisite of the *ollamh dána* of a territory was the right to take as a fee the wedding garments of every woman married within it. This has been shown to be a very ancient survival with analogies in early Indo-European custom.[5]

Military groupings

English writers of the sixteenth century divide the Irish fighting men into three classes: horsemen, galloglass and kerne. Of these only the galloglass could be described as purely professional soldiers, for while there were full-time horsemen and kerne in the service of the great lords, the able-bodied population of the country, when called out for service in the general 'rising-out' or levy of the country, served, according to their means, as horsemen or kerne. The galloglass, on the other hand, were salaried professionals. The obligation to serve in the 'rising-out' or general hosting (*gairmsluaigh*) was universal, only the clergy and the Gaelic learned classes being exempt. The 1598 survey of Mac Carthy Mór's tributes declares that every able-bodied man was bound to answer the summons with sufficient weapons and supplied with three days victuals, and that default incurred a fine of twenty shillings. In the adjacent palatinate of Kerry the horseman who failed to appear paid a fine of three cows, or fifteen shillings in lieu; the kerne only one cow, or five shillings. The obligation to take up arms in defence of one's country – or its rulers – is a universal one and one would expect to find it, as one does, in medieval Ireland, but the 1598 Mac Carthy survey pinpoints the inevitable qualification of all Irish institutions when it adds: 'but such of the country as were his [Mac Carthy Mór's] enemies would never yield to any such rising'. It would be an exceptionally powerful or exceptionally fortunate chief who would not find his summons ignored by a substantial part of his subjects, who might well, indeed, be ready instead to take part with any invader.

The Irish horseman of the sixteenth century was a

remarkable illustration of the way in which an inefficient or obsolete practice can not only survive but actually extend itself at the expense of a more efficient one; for during the fourteenth and fifteenth centuries the Irish manner of riding – like other Gaelic customs – had been adopted not only by the totally Gaelicised elements but also – to the distress of the Dublin administration – by the borderers of the Pale itself. In the early years of the sixteenth century Sir William Darcy could boast that he was the only man on the borders of Meath who still rode in the English fashion, that is to say, with stirrups. For the Irish horseman, eight hundred years behind the rest of Europe, still rode without them, thereby rendering himself of little value as a fighting unit. Unable, for want of stirrups, to couch a lance, he carried the javelin which was his principal weapon overarm in the ancient manner. The other equipment of the Irish horseman is well known from contemporary drawings. His saddle was a stuffed cushion, held in place by a breast-strap and breeching as well as a girth, while his bit – in contrast to the severe curb used by his English contemporary – was a plain snaffle, usually of brass. Besides his javelin, he carried a sword and dagger, and was equipped with a helmet and with either a mail-shirt or a 'jack' of quilted leather, sufficient to turn the blow of a sword. This equipment had not changed substantially between 1397 and the late sixteenth century. The horseman had always two horses, often three, each with its groom or 'horseboy' in attendance; these horseboys also took part in battles as light troops. The horsemen were recruited from the richer and more prosperous elements of the landowning classes, while the poorer sections of the latter would have been obliged to serve as kerne.

The kerne (Gaelic *ceithearn* or *ceithearnach*, Latin *turbarius*) is perhaps better thought of less as a specific type of soldier than as the ordinary able-bodied freemen who, although unable to afford the horse and mail of a horseman, bore arms as a matter of course. At its earliest appearance, however, in the late thirteenth and early fourteenth centuries, the word seems definitely to have been applied to the members of mercenary bands serving under great Anglo-Norman lords. It might be hazarded that the personnel of these bands were recruited from the Gaelic land-owning classes displaced by the Norman settlement, but this is pure speculation. In later days these bands of professional kerne in the service of a lord were known as kernety (*ceitheirn tighe*) or household kerne (*per contra*, *ceithearn coille* or 'wood-kerne' signified a bandit); they play an important part in the Ormond territories and elsewhere from the early fifteenth century on. The captains of these bands of household kerne seem to have been usually hereditary. The 'Keating kerne' captained by and largely recruited from the Keating family served the earl of Kildare. After the fall of the Kildares in 1534 they passed, like the Kildare's galloglass, into the service of the Crown, and – again like the galloglass – were to play an important role in the plantation of Leix in the 1560s, although at that date the restored earl of Kildare had 160 'Keating kerne' in his service, which he quartered by coyne and livery upon the inhabitants of County Kildare and of the adjacent parts of Meath, for whose defence they were ostensibly maintained. Another branch of the Keatings served as captains of kerne in County Tipperary.

The kerne were without armour; their equipment was either a sword and target, a bow (the Irish bow was only about half the length of the English longbow) and arrows, or a set of three javelins, which they hurled at the enemy with great skill. After the use of hand-firearms had become general in the sixteenth century many of the kerne graduated to their use, and these were the 'shot' whom we find mentioned in the records of the time of

O Neill's wars. The wages of a kerne in 1575 were a heifer, worth 8 shillings, for the quarter of the year, besides his provisions during the period; the captain of a hundred hired kerne in fact provided only 92, the wages and provisions of the remaining eight 'black men' constituting his own salary.

The use of siege engines is mentioned often enough in the Irish annals to show that it was a normal practice. When in 1478 Rory Mac Dermot besieged the then Mac Dermot, whom he was seeking to depose, in the Rock of Lough Key he sent for skilled workmen from Fermanagh to construct siege engines. These seem to have cast arrows as well as, or instead of, stones. In 1527 we hear of a great 'sow', a kind of shed made of great beams of oak and mounted on wheels, under the protection of which the walls could be undermined, being used in the siege of a castle in County Roscommon. By this time, however, the use of siege artillery, which seems to have been first employed in Ireland by the Kildares, was already spreading. The use of smaller firearms came in at the same time or shortly after, and was already general by the middle of the century; it must have played its part in the increasing violence and desolation of the sixteenth century.

The galloglass

The galloglass, as is well known, were a class of professional mercenary soldiers with a distinctive weapon – the spar or galloglass axe – and a distinctive way of fighting, who played a prominent part in the affairs of fourteenth, fifteenth and sixteenth-century Ireland. The term galloglass (*gallóglach*), which literally signifies 'foreign warrior', first appears in the second half of the thirteenth century to denote the Scottish mercenaries, recruited from the mixed Gaelic and Scandinavian population of the Western Isles, who then begin to appear in the service of the Irish

kings of the north and west. During the last quarter of
the thirteenth and the whole of the fourteenth century a
steady stream of recruits continued to arrive in Ireland,
drawn from the defeated factions in the internal wars
of the Isles and the western Highlands. After 1400,
however, recruitment from the Highlands seems to have
almost – though probably not entirely – dried up, and,
as Hayes-McCoy has demonstrated, the galloglass must
be carefully distinguished from a quite different class of
Scottish mercenary, the 'redshanks' of the sixteenth
century. These later arrivals made no permanent settlements, while the galloglass – though they continued until
the end to be known in Latin as *scotici* – were from the
beginning naturalised in Ireland. The Mac Sweenys had
established themselves as territorial lords in Tirconnell
before 1300 – the three Mac Sweeny chiefs were bound
to serve their overlord, O Donnell, with fixed contingents
of galloglass. The Mac Donnell galloglass of Tyrone,
who served O Neill, also possessed a territory called by
English writers of the late sixteenth century 'the galloglass
country', around Ballygawley in Tyrone. In most areas,
however, the acquisition of land – by pledge or otherwise
– by the galloglass septs seems not to have begun until
well on in the sixteenth century. The great galloglass
captains – 'five brethren and the sons of two other
brethren of one lineage, called McSwynes' – whom Sir
Henry Sidney met at Cork in 1576 were landless men –
although 'of such credit and force they would make the
greatest lords of the province both in fear of them and
glad of their friendship' – and their ancestors had been
settled in Munster for two or three generations. Sometimes the galloglass would take lands in pledge for their
unpaid bonnaght.

Two of the greatest galloglass stocks, the Mac Sweenys
and Mac Donnells, have been already mentioned. The
Mac Sweenys spread from Tirconnell into Connacht,

where they became by the end of the fourteenth century the galloglass arm of the faction headed by Clanrickard, as the Mac Donnells and Mac Dowells were of that headed by the Lower Mac William (see Chapter VIII). From Connacht they passed into the service of the O Briens of Thomond, the Butlers of Ormond, and the Mac Carthys of Desmond and Carbery. In the early sixteenth century they seem to have been identified with hostility to the Geraldines, and the marriage-contract of Donald Mac Carthy Reagh with Kildare's daughter Eleanor (1513) provided for their banishment from Carbery. When the eighth and ninth earls of Kildare recruited galloglass it was to the Mac Donnells of County Mayo that they sent. After the fall of the Kildares in 1534 these galloglass passed into the service of the Crown, and we find the Mac Donnell galloglass in the royal service during the remainder of the century. The Mac Sheehys, who claimed to be related to the Mac Donnells, provided galloglass for the earls of Desmond.

The battle equipment of the galloglass consisted of a long mailcoat and a helmet, a dagger and their peculiar weapon, the galloglass axe or 'spar', a heavy, long-handled battle-axe or halbert. Every galloglass was accompanied by a manservant who carried his mailcoat when he was not in action, and by a boy who carried his provisions and cooked for him. The unit of three persons thus formed was called, after the axe which the galloglass carried, a 'spar' and a nominal 100 or 120 spars made up a 'battle' (i.e. battalion) of galloglass. In fact, the nominal hundred only amounted in fact to 80 or 87 spars (the number varies in different accounts, probably on account of local variations of practice) the remainder being 'black' or non-existent men whose pay and victuals were drawn by the captain ('constable') of the band as salary. The galloglass were normally hired by the quarter, although very great lords maintained bands on a more or less permanent basis, billeting them on different parts of their territory in each quarter of the year. The constable of a band, besides the benefit of his 'black men', was customarily given for the quarter's hire of his band a present of a war-horse and a hack.

Out of a band of galloglass, only a very small proportion would have belonged to the recognised galloglass septs; Robert Cowley in 1537 wrote contemptuously that 'amongst 200 of them there shall be scant eight that be gentlemen and look like to able men, and all the residue slaves . . . gathered out of divers countries'. He also suggests that the captains, who were accustomed to keep a supply of mailcoats to equip these recruits, would sometimes hire them on the cheap and pocket the difference. Such hastily summoned and underpaid recruits could hardly have lived up to the traditional fighting repute of the galloglass, which stood high, although Sir Nicholas Malby in 1578 describes them as 'mostly cowards'. (He was, however, arguing for their replacement in the Queen's service by English troops.) Dymmok, writing around 1600, declares that 'the galloglass are picked and selected men of great and mighty bodies, cruel without compassion, . . . choosing rather to die than to yield the field, so that when it cometh to handy [i.e. hand-to-hand] blows, they are quickly [either] slain or win the field'. An earlier account of 1534 says 'these sort of men be those that do not lightly abandon the field, but bide the brunt to the death', and there are instances in the annals of whole battalions of galloglass so perishing together in defeat. It seems certain, in spite of such criticisms as Cowley's, that the galloglass in general must have possessed a remarkable esprit-de-corps. The cess or quartering of the galloglass on the country bore the technical name of bonnaght (*buannacht*), a word which appears frequently in sixteenth-century records. The bonnaght was one of the most onerous of the Irish impositions.

5 The Church and Clergy in Society

The Irish Church

In the six centuries between the original evangelisation of Ireland and the year 1100, the Irish Church had developed its own peculiar pattern in virtual isolation, with the result that a pattern of organisation had emerged quite distinct from that prevalent in western Christendom as a whole. Most conspicuous of these peculiarities of organisation were the absence of a territorial episcopate – which had existed, at least in embryo, in the earliest stage but had subsequently disappeared, its organisation on the basis of monastic *paruchiae* – chains of smaller establishments dependent on a great foundation, such as Clonmacnois or Derry, and its acceptance of the principle of hereditary succession – of the usual Irish kind by seniority – to ecclesiastical office which had insensibly transformed the former monastic establishments into collegiate foundations for the benefit of a particular clan. Most strikingly, as has been pointed out, the Irish Church had never succeeded in extending beyond the purely religious sphere, and such a matter as marriage remained in Ireland a purely secular concern. The reformers of the twelfth century sought to bring Ireland into line with the general practice of Christendom, establishing a diocesan episcopate and introducing the new religious orders of western Europe, such as the Cistercians. These were the first reforms to be accepted; they were to be followed by the enforcement of the payment of tithes and by the establishment of a parochial system. In these respects the reformers were able to bring Ireland into line with general European practice; in others they were to be less successful. We have seen how they totally failed to bring marriage and family life into the Christian pattern, while the pattern of a hereditary clergy, which they had fought so vigorously, was to persevere and after 1400 to invade even the new religious orders, such as the Cistercians and Premonstratensians.

The clergy

The most striking feature, at first sight, of the Irish clergy in the later middle ages was the strongly hereditary character of the profession, although this can be paralleled from other outlying parts of Europe (especially the other Celtic lands of Scotland and Wales) where attempts to enforce the rule of clerical celibacy had been largely ineffective. The customs of hereditary succession – understanding the term to mean succession by election within the family, in the Irish manner, and not primogeniture succession from father to son – and of a married clergy had of course been two of the 'abuses' of the Irish Church most strongly attacked by the twelfth-century reformers. The practice survived well into the thirteenth century; down to the middle of that century the diocese of Killala with all its benefices remained the almost undisputed property of its great ecclesiastical family of O Maoilfhaghmhair, while at a lower level and even in the most occupied area, we find the church of Leixlip passing from a priest to his son soon after 1200. In 1250 the bishop of Ossory was to complain to the pope against the prevalence of hereditary succession in the churches of his diocese. It would have seemed, however, that the practice was doomed to disappear, for the adoption of the rule of clerical celibacy meant that the sons of the clergy were by definition illegitimate, and according to the developed canon law, which at this time was assuming its definitive form, the illegitimate were debarred from ecclesiastical office without special papal dispensation, which seems to have been sparingly granted.

The accession of Pope John XXII in 1316 was to lead to a total reversal of this trend towards the elimination of the hereditary clerical families which the doctrine of clerical celibacy was bringing about. For the pressing financial commitments of the Avignon papacy necessitated new methods of raising money, and one of the easiest and most obvious ways was the sale of dispensations. The avenue of ecclesiastical promotion was once more freely open to the sons of the clergy, provided they could pay the necessary fees at Rome or Avignon to secure release from the disabilities imposed on them by the strict letter of the canon law, and it is to be noted that it is with the reign of John XXII that it again becomes normal to find the sons of clerics following in their fathers' profession. Master John O Grady, Archbishop of Cashel 1332–45, was the father of another John, Archbishop of Tuam 1365–71, who in turn was the father of a third John, Bishop of Elphin (d.1417). The O Gradys do not seem to have produced another bishop, although they continued to follow the clerical profession; the bishop's son Nicholas, chief of his name and coarb of Tuamgreny, was the father of at least two beneficed sons; the elder of these, a canon of Killaloe, was the father of Sir Donogh Óg O Grady, provided as archdeacon of the diocese in 1528 and who died, 'a lord in church and state', in 1558. In 1567 one of his sons was claiming the archdeaconry of Killaloe by provision, and another the deanery, in each case against rival candidates. In most cases, however, lack of adequate information makes it impossible to work out the exact relationships of these ecclesiastical families. An ecclesiastical family of whom we can fortunately give a coherent picture is the branch of the Maguires known as the Sliocht Lachtláin. Maurice Maguire, archdeacon of Clogher and rector of Aghalurcher, known as 'the Great Archdeacon', died in 1423 and his wife Joan, daughter of Bishop Mac Cawell of Clogher (Brian, who had died in 1358) in 1427, 'after fifty-six years hospitable housekeeping at Cleenish' (where her husband had held the family erenaghship of part of the church lands). Besides daughters, they had had four sons. The eldest, John, a Master of Arts, who was rector of Devenish, predeceased his father, leaving a son who became rector of Magheracoolmoney. The archdeacon's second son, Pierse, born when his father was already in priest's orders, studied canon and civil law for three years at Oxford and for seven years at private schools in Ireland. He became rector of Iniskeen and canon of Clogher, then archdeacon of Clogher in succession to his father and eventually, in 1433, bishop of the see. He resigned his bishopric in 1448 and died (in a crannog at the family home of Cleenish) in 1450. The third son of the great archdeacon, Thomas Maguire, was abbot of Lisgoole; the *Annals of Ulster* in 1419 record the death of 'the mother of [his] children'. He seems to have resigned his abbacy in favour of a nephew, Brian, 'the young abbot', whose father had been the archdeacon's fourth son. A son of the 'young abbot' by a married woman was Redmond Maguire, prior of Lisgoole, who died in 1522. Bishop Pierse was the father of at least four sons; William, the eldest was canon of Clogher and afterwards, like his uncle and cousin, abbot of Lisgoole. On his death in 1483 he was succeeded, after some intriguing at Rome for the position, by a Laurence Maguire who is described as being son of a former abbot (either Thomas or Brian) and who held the abbacy until his death in 1527. Abbot William had several children, of whose careers we know nothing, but it is at least possible that one of them, Philip, murdered in County Louth in 1492, was the Philip

Maguire who became archdeacon in 1472, and was afterwards removed, restored and removed again. Two other sons of Bishop Pierse were Edmond, born when his father was a priest, who became rector of Cleenish and dean of Clogher, exchanging that dignity for the archdeaconry in 1454, and dying in 1471, and John, rector of Derrymullan, who succeeded his brother Edmond in the family erenaghship of Cleenish. A later member of the family was Redmond Maguire, vicar of Cleenish, who was son of one of the archdeacons mentioned above and who died in 1534. Bishop Pierse had resigned his see in favour of Ross Maguire, a son of the ruling lord of Fermanagh, Thomas Óg, and Bishop Ross, who died in 1483, was also to found an ecclesiastical branch of the family. Of his seven sons John was canon of Clogher and rector of Aghalurcher; the *Annals of Ulster*, on his death in 1501, praise him as a man skilled in both foreign and Gaelic learning, as well as in lay accomplishments. He was father of Brian Maguire, also rector of Aghalurcher, slain in 1529 when trying to make peace between two warring groups. Other sons of Bishop Ross were Hugh, rector of Cleenish and (in succession to his brother) of Aghalurcher and rural dean of Lough Erne, and Donnell, who made a bid for the abbacy of Clones in 1497 but died soon after. Turlough, 'son of the Bishop Maguire', who was prior of Lough Derg and rector of Derrymullan and died through falling down a staircase at Athboy, County Meath, in 1504, was probably a son of Bishop Ross rather than of Bishop Pierse.

Such patterns were in no way exceptional. Murtough ('Maurice') O Kelly, bishop of Clonfert and afterwards (1393–1407) archbishop of Tuam, had four sons, only one of whom is not known to have followed his father's profession. The second son Thomas became, like his father, bishop of Clonfert and was promoted to Tuam shortly before his death in 1441, though he never took possession of the archbishopric. The fourth, Connor, born during his father's episcopate in Clonfert, entered the Cistercian abbey of Knockmoy, of which he became abbot. Bishop Thomas during his episcopate begot at least two sons: one became rector of Athenry and the other archdeacon of Clonfert. But besides this general tendency of the sons of the clergy to become clerics, the papal registers of the fifteenth century are full of examples of sons directly succeeding their fathers in benefices, either by papal dispensation or by means of such devices as collusive lawsuits, etc. designed to evade the canon law prohibition against this form of hereditary succession. On the death of their dean Donogh O Carolan in 1367, the chapter of Derry elected in his place his (legitimate) son Master Pierse O Carolan, chancellor of Armagh. Dermot O Lonergan, dean of Killaloe, who died *circa* 1418, was succeeded, by provision, by his son James. In 1460 Bartholomew O Flanagan, Augustinian prior of Devenish, resigned his priorship in favour of his son Laurence (born during his father's tenure as prior), who held it until his death in 1505.

In some cases these sons of clerics were technically legitimate (like Dean Pierse O Carolan mentioned above), having been born before their fathers' entry into major orders. In any case, one must not be misled by the slanted term 'concubine' into thinking that the partners of the clergy were of inferior social status. In that most clerical of the later annals, the *Annals of Ulster*, (drawn up, in part, by a cleric who was the father of at least fourteen children), their obits are entered like those of other gentry and notables. The wives of Thomas Mac Cormaic O Donnell and Connor Mac Cormaic O Donnell, bishops of Raphoe (1319–37 and 1367–97) were the daughters, respectively, of Mac Sweeny and O Boyle, two of the greatest lords in the diocese. Mahon, 'the Young Bishop' O Brien of Kilmacduagh (1503–32) – a son of Turlough, bishop of Killaloe (1483–1526) – married his kinswoman Ranelt, the daughter of Turlough O Brien, lord of Thomond, and their son Turlough (II), bishop of Killaloe 1556–69, married his cousin, another Ranelt, the daughter of the first earl of Thomond.

Clerical marriage was of course in theory strictly forbidden by the church, and late medieval Ireland did not lack reformers ready to point this out and to denounce it as an abuse. In 1442–3 an unknown writer addressed a tract on the subject, replete with a wealth of quotations from canon law, to Manus Mac Mahon, tanist of Oriel, urging him to suppress clerical marriage within the area under his rule. Provincial synods, such as those of Armagh in 1426 and 1449 and that of Cashel in 1453 (and no doubt many others as well) legislated against the practice, commanding the clergy to separate from their wives within one month of being warned to do so, under pain of excommunication and deprivation. The exact effects of such decrees, bearing in mind the typical medieval gap between theory and practice, is doubtful. We may look at them in the light of similar contemporaneous decrees against such abuses as lay taxation of church lands and the 'naming' (see Chapter IV) of children. It is unlikely that they would have been totally without result, but their effect could only have been transient. A visitation made in 1546 of the rural deanery of Tullaghoge (County Tyrone), which gives a precious glimpse of the ecclesiastical condition of a Gaelic area at that period, shows some of the clergy as 'concubinary' and others as not, but in the case of at least two priests returned under the latter heading the visitors admit that their late 'concubines' were still present in the neighbourhood, leading one to suspect that the separation had only been effected for the period of the visitation. As in contemporary Wales, it is probable that a little discreet bribery of his bishop and archdeacon, who themselves were probably in the same condition as himself, was in most cases sufficient to protect the married priest from officious molestation. If he was liable to delation at Rome by a rival covetous of his benefice, the same thing was true in many other cases, and in any case the facts alleged by the delator were less important than the influence either party could bring to bear to secure a favourable decision in the consequent lawsuit. Lochlann or Laurence O Gallagher II, bishop of Raphoe (1442–78), himself the grandson of a former bishop and whom we know to have been the father of at least seven sons (of whom four at least held benefices), was denounced in 1469 for various offences, principally fornication, and suspended, but he seems to have had little difficulty in securing either absolution from his metropolitan, John Bole of Armagh, or acquittal by a court at Rome (1476), though we do not know what the process cost him in bribes. It seems a likely supposition that the primates of Armagh, always Englishmen, Palesmen or foreigners, were less tolerant of such behaviour than their purely Irish counterparts elsewhere.

Clerical life

Medieval Ireland never acquired a university, a defect most probably to be attributed to its political disorder rather than to the poverty of the country, if we may take the very different experience of Scotland as a guide. In consequence Irish clerics who wished to obtain degrees had to go to universities abroad, although a thorough grounding in the civil and canon laws could be obtained in private schools in Ireland. Canon law, which not only opened the way to a lucrative practice in the Church courts but also was of immediate practical value to the cleric seeking to litigate for a benefice, was the normal choice of study – as the writer of 1515 says; 'the Church of this land use not to learn any other science but the law of canon, for covetousness of lucre transitory; all other science, whereof grow none such lucre, the persons of the church do despise'. The study of theology was in general left to the friars, who maintained their own schools for the purpose. The favourite university of the Irish was Oxford, and an English statute of 1413 directed against Irish students seems to have had little effect in cutting down the numbers of Irish who attended it. The Irish at Oxford, though, provided not only students but teachers as well; 'the Great Master' Mathew O Howen, son of an archdeacon of Clogher, lectured at Oxford for fourteen years. (It is perhaps symptomatic of the Irish conditions mentioned above that we learn this from his wife's obit (1382) in the *Annals of Ulster*.) Other Irish clerics went further afield, to Cambridge or to Bologna and other continental universities, and in the late sixteenth century we find a number of clerics from the northern dioceses of Derry and Raphoe attending the Scottish university of Glasgow. But in general most Irish clerics gained their education 'according to the custom of the country' in local schools (*studia particularia*) at home, or combined this with a shorter period spent at a university; Pierse Maguire, afterwards bishop of Clogher, had studied three years at Oxford and seven years in local schools. A decree of the synod of Limerick (1453) forbade the teachers in such schools to admit nobles and other laymen to their lectures, unless they had good reason to believe that they intended to adopt a clerical career.

If foreign universities drew Irish clerics as students, Rome, the fount of papal favours and provisions to benefices, drew them even more strongly as seekers for promotion. Of course not every seeker for a benefice went to Rome; the majority were certainly content to be represented by their agents, but a large number certainly went in person. The climate or the local diseases, for fifteenth-century Rome was notoriously unhealthy, seem to have often proved fatal to the newly-arrived; in 1444 a large number of Connacht and Ulster clergy, who had gone to Rome in company with William O Hedian, bishop of Elphin, died there, although the bishop himself survived. There were Irish clerks employed by the curia in the first half of the fifteenth century at least, but we know little of the doings of the considerable Irish colony which must have existed in Rome. A note in the *Annals of Ulster* on the death (1466) of Teig Duff Mac Gillacoisgle, 'who took the eric of Cuchulainn from the Connachtmen in Rome', suggests a rowdy kind of inter-provincial feuding among the Irish there, and one would like to know more about this episode.

Like the clergy of every other European country in the later medieval period, Irish clergy were being constantly reproved by synods for wearing lay dress instead of that proper to their profession, with little effect. A constant cause of complaint in Ireland was their wearing of long hair and moustaches, the normal Irish fashion but both disapproved for clerics. A more serious form of laicisation was when the clergy took part in secular wars and battles. In 1444 Cormac Mac Coghlan, bishop of Clonmacnois, was slain in a battle with a rival faction of Mac Coghlans, to whom he had previously refused a truce even of a day or a night. With him fell his son, archdeacon of the diocese, his two brothers and the prior of Clontuskert, his ally. The circumstances of his death did not prevent the annalist who recorded it from invoking 'God's blessing and the blessing of all saints and true Christians with that bishop to his terrestial [*sic*] mansion,' for 'a common giver to all the clergy of Ireland, and a special true friend to all the learned in the Irish liberal sciences also was that eminent Lord Bishop.' Many other warlike bishops occur in the records. William O Farrell of Ardagh (1480–1516) and Richard Barret of Killala (1513–44) combined the episcopal office with that of secular lord and chief of their name. The latter, when his opponents on one occasion placed their cattle in sanctuary in the famous termon of Errew, personally took them out of it to deliver to their pursuers, his allies.

Still worse, however, than the involvement of the clergy in secular wars was when wars and murders took place over the succession to ecclesiastical benefices. In 1435 Bishop O Connell of Killala, whose diocese was divided politically between the lordships of the Barrets and of the O Dowdas, was driven from his see – in spite of armed support from the Barret faction – by the O Dowdas, who installed the archdeacon, an O Dowda, who had been elected as anti-bishop by some of the chapter, in his place. Bishop O Connell went to Rome to obtain papal intervention, and, his rival having died soon after, was enabled to return without opposition. In 1461, however, he was murdered by the sons of the late archdeacon, one of whom, a cleric, subsequently obtained papal rehabilitation on the grounds that he and his brother had not intended to murder their bishop but only to steal his horses! The dispute between William Roche and Gerald Fitz Gerald over the united sees of Cork and Cloyne led in 1484 to the former and his five sons bringing an army which sacked and burned the town of Cloyne. In 1476 the dean of Elphin, O Mochan, was slain in a dispute over the deanery.

With clerics engaging in warfare among themselves as well as taking part in secular wars, it is little wonder that towards the end of the period we find a growing disregard for the privileges of sanctuary and immunity claimed by the Church for its possessions. Breaches of these immunities had constantly occurred, and the Church had found it necessary to re-proclaim them under the penalty of excommunication on many occasions, as in Clogher after the issuing of the bull *Clericis laicos* in 1297 and at the provincial synod of Cashel held at Limerick in 1453, with what effect we cannot say. But in the sixteenth century we find an increasing disregard for these claims. Great lords like the earl of Desmond levied coyne and livery from the clerics within their jurisdiction just as they did from their lay subjects (though the lords of Gaelic Ulster seem to have refrained to some degree in this respect), while even the most famous termons failed to afford sanctuary against violence, and were often the subject of violence themselves.

Papal provisions

According to the doctrine of the fully developed canon law, the right of appointment of the clergy was inherently vested in the bishop as part of his 'ordinary' episcopal jurisdiction. In practice, the custom of lay patronage ('advowson') was too deeply entrenched in feudal Europe for the Church to suppress it, or even attempt seriously to do so. In England, where resistance to clerical claims was especially strong, the official canon law doctrines on the subject received little recognition and where the bishop made an appointment this tended to be regarded as an exercise of a right of advowson vested in himself. In Ireland no parochial system had existed, outside the towns of the Ostmen, before the invasion of 1169, and the formation of parishes was a long-drawn-out process over the following century and a quarter, the period during which the canon law was taking its final formulated shape. In consequence the pattern of patronage in Ireland tends to vary according to the date at which the parochial system took shape in that particular region. In the east the English pattern was in general prevalent, but in Munster and Connacht – where parochial formation dated from the first half of the thirteenth century – we find the curious compromise, noted in later times as peculiarly Irish, by which although the sinecure rectory was of lay patronage or vested in a monastery, the vicar who actually performed the duties was 'collated' (appointed) by the bishop. In Gaelic Ulster, where the parishes were of still later origin and where there were no Norman lords to claim the right of advowson – the Gaelic lords rarely did so – both rectors and vicars (for it was the custom everywhere for each parish to have both a sinecure rectory, usually held by some student or scholar, and a vicarage) were collated by the bishops.

By canon law doctrine the pope was 'universal ordinary' and could override the bishops on any matter within their jurisdiction, including ecclesiastical appointments. The earlier and most notorious employment of this right was to secure rich benefices for absentee curial officials and relatives of the pope, a practice which aroused great hostility everywhere and which led in England from 1353 onwards to the passing of the various Statutes of Provisors and of Praemunire. The poverty of most Irish benefices and the chaotic condition of the country, which would have made it impossible for an absentee to draw any sort of revenue from it, protected Ireland from this abuse. The kind of provision which we find in Gaelic and Gaelicised Ireland, and with which we are concerned here, was of a different kind, in which a suppliant would petition the pope for appointment to a benefice. This kind of appointment only began to become common towards the close of the fourteenth century, and its great surge forward dated from the pontificate of Martin V (1417–31). From that time the stream of Irish petitioners rapidly became a flood. Even in the 1560s, after the accession of Elizabeth I but before the new Church order had been imposed over most of the country – and it is salutary to remember that the last bishop recognised by both pope and crown, Owen O Hart of Achonry, did not die until 1603 – large numbers of Irishmen were still seeking provisions at Rome. Bulls for Irishmen were often or even usually expedited *gratis*, without payment of the usual fees, on account of their poverty, a practice which must have increased the number of applicants.

The benefice petitioned for by the applicant might be one which had fallen to papal appointment for some reason (such as the death of the previous holder at Rome or his promotion to a bishopric, both of which gave the curia the right of filling the vacancy; again, whole classes of benefices might be reserved for papal provision by special decree or it might be one actually occupied, the holder being denounced by the petitioner as guilty of various crimes or as having obtained it without legal right. As was observed by the great medievalist G. G. Coulton, the 'common informer' or delator of this type makes a sudden appearance in Irish and Scots ecclesiastical affairs with the accession of Martin V, and thereafter a steady stream of such denunciations poured in to Rome. The charges made by the delators might well be and probably usually were true, but as Coulton remarks, the practice was not the way to bring about reforms, and in any case the delators were themselves certainly no better. Delations might be collusive; thus it was common practice for a son to evade the canon law rule which forbade him to directly succeed his father in his benefice by denouncing his father as detaining the benefice in question without legal right and obtaining a provision himself. As the father's occupancy had been declared void, the son was not in theory succeeding him. Provisions to delators – and this, as has been often emphasised, was true of most papal provisions – were not of course absolute but were subject to the proviso 'if the facts be as stated', but as the judges ('delegates') who were nominated by the bull to determine the facts seem to have been normally chosen by the petitioner it is reasonable to suppose that he chose persons likely to be favourable to him. In any case, the prospect of interminable litigation on an appointment did not worry the clerks who issued it. In the sixteenth century, with declining standards, they seem to have become quite reckless in this matter, conflicting provisions to the same benefice being issued within a few days of each other.

As has been remarked, the poverty of Ireland secured its immunity from one abuse of papal provision, the appointment of absentees. The indiscriminate granting of provisions did, however, lead in Ireland to another abuse which was to have serious consequences for the Irish church. During the second half of the fifteenth century it became the practice to grant provisions to members of great and influential families who were barely in minor orders or were even still laymen but had declared their intention to take orders. In the sixteenth century this practice became more and more widespread. Theoretically, such a provision would be subsequently rendered invalid by the failure of the provisor to take orders, but in fact when a great man had secured possession of an abbey or benefice no power existed which could effectively secure his removal. In 1533 Rory or Gilladuff O Shaughnessy, afterwards lord of Kinelea (died 1569), secured a provision to the deanery of Kilmacduagh; he was still detaining its revenues in 1567, to the exclusion of the nominal dean, a genuine cleric. He seems to have been illiterate. It was no doubt against persons of this type that King Henry VIII's ordinances of 1541 were directed when they decreed that no lord should usurp any vacant benefices without collation, admission by the 'ordinary' and canonical institution. The great monasteries, because of their wealth, were especially liable to be taken over by commendators of this type.

The monastic orders

Little of the earlier forms of Celtic monasticism had survived the twelfth-century reforms. Two or three communities of culdees survived in the north and a number of the older monastic establishments, such as Derry, had evolved into houses of Augustinian Canons Regular. In general, however, the establishments of the earlier age of Irish monasticism had by the late medieval period become simply ecclesiastical possessions held under the bishops by clans of hereditary coarbs and erenaghs (see below).

The twelfth-century reforms brought into Ireland the monastic orders of contemporary Europe. The introduction of the Cistercian order into Ireland was the work of St Malachy of Armagh. The Cistercian houses were new foundations unconnected with any existing ecclesiastical establishments, but those of Gaelic foundation, headed by Mellifont, soon developed many peculiarly Irish features of discipline and life irreconcilable with normal Cistercian practice. After 1216 the attempt by the authorities of the order to bring them into line with the general practice, exacerbated by racial feeling – for the visitors who sought to impose the reform were Englishmen and were supported by the monasteries of English affiliation founded by the Anglo-Norman invaders – led to a struggle in which the Gaelic houses – who had resisted in some cases by force of arms – were in 1228 forced to submit and brought under control. It was not until 1274, at the instance of that great and nationalistically-minded Irishman, David Mac Carroll, archbishop of Cashel, that they to some degree recovered their autonomy. The Cistercian houses of English foundation, like some others of other orders, were often violently hostile to the native Irish, whom they were in many cases forbidden by their statutes to receive as monks. The 'remonstrance' of the Irish to Pope John XXII in 1318 declared that the Cistercian monks of Granard (Abbeylara) and of Inch openly declared it no sin to kill an Irishman, and would even celebrate mass after doing so.

During the fourteenth century, a complete reorientation

took place in the religious houses, geographical situation becoming the decisive factor. The great Gaelic Cistercian house of Mellifont (which as late as 1321 had been refusing to admit Englishmen as monks) became through its position in the Pale purely English, while conversely the violently anti-Gaelic Granard was in 1400 forced by the pope to pass over its own statutes and admit Irish monks; within eleven years it was a purely Gaelic house and the abbacy a prerogative of the O Farrells. On the other hand, the priory of Killaha in Kerry obtained in 1402 papal confirmation of the rule laid down by its founder, the justiciar Geoffrey de Mareis, that only persons of English descent should be admitted. It would be unwise to see in these contrary examples the survival of earlier racial animosity; both can more likely be explained in terms of a struggle for control between rival local clans. The exclusiveness of Killaha regarding descent had disappeared by 1484.

In the Gaelic and Gaelicised area the monasteries had by 1400 already ceased to live a conventual life according to their rules and were assuming a form not unlike that of the Irish ecclesiastical establishments before the twelfth-century reforms, but complicated by the rules of the new game of papal provision and delation at Rome (see above). The abbots and their monks, like the secular clergy, abandoned all pretence of celibacy and openly married. In 1397 Primate Colton of Armagh, conducting a visitation of the diocese of Derry in the vacancy of that see, commanded Abbot Hugh Mac Gilbride of Derry to separate from his wife within three days, forbidding him to pay her the settlement (*coibhche* or bride-price, see Chapter IV) he had agreed to make and further forbidding him to make or promise any such settlement to any other woman he might in the future take as 'concubine', while both he and his canons were forbidden to spend the goods of the house on any woman. In 1466 the Premonstratensian abbey of Lough Key was accidentally burned by a canon's wife carrying a lighted candle. With married monks it was not surprising that, as was sometimes complained, they did not live in the monasteries but scattered through the neighbouring countryside. Abbacies and priorships came to be treated as simple ecclesiastical benefices, and like other benefices became quasi-hereditary in particular families. Cormac Mac David, made abbot of Boyle by the abbot of Mellifont in 1414, was the son (born during his father's abbacy) of a previous abbot, Donagh Mac David (died 1383). Dermot O Heffernan, Cistercian abbot of Holycross in the mid-fifteenth century, was the son of a previous abbot, Ferrall O Heffernan, and the father of Maurice O Heffernan, abbot of another Cistercian house, Inishlawnaught. Ambitious clerics transferred from one order to another whenever a chance of promotion presented itself.

As the fifteenth century progressed, the secularisation of the monasteries became worse, as less and less clerically-inclined superiors were provided by the pope. In a well-known report to the central authorities of the Cistercian order on the condition of the order in Ireland, around 1498, the abbot of Mellifont declares that many of those provided never took orders, but continued to live as lay noblemen, simply drawing the revenues of their abbeys. In none of the houses outside the Pale, he declares, was the Cistercian rule observed or its habit worn. When he himself had attempted to conduct a visitation of some of these houses he had been resisted by force by the commendators in possession – just as the Irish Cistercian houses had resisted an earlier visitation in the 1220s – who had garrisoned the abbeys with armed men to resist him, and he asked to be excused from conducting such visitations in future. The Gaelic commendators of the late fifteenth and sixteenth centuries – like their contemporaries in Scotland – were purely secular figures, to whom their monasteries were simply sources of revenue. Their attitude is well displayed in the simoniacal agreement by which William O Dwyer, abbot of Holycross, surrendered his abbacy to Philip Purcell in 1534. The resigning abbot was to have a third of the goods and crops of the abbey, with certain lands and grazings and a third of the offerings made to the famous relic of the holy cross (from which the abbey took its name) during his life. Like any secular agreement, the document names (lay) arbitrators in case of disagreement and persons who were to act as *sláinte* (see Chapter III) for its observance, these latter including Purcell's brother, the baron of Loughmoe, and the sons of Abbot O Dwyer himself. Glaisne Magennis combined the Cistercian abbacy of Newry with the priorship of the Benedictines of Down and of the Augustinians of Saul, and used this concentration of landed wealth to further his own political power in the area; he fell at the hands of his own nephews in 1527. Rory Mac Dermot (died 1568) was abbot of the Premonstratensians of Lough Key for sixty years, during the last nineteen of which he was also ruling lord of Moylurg. His obit, which occupies three pages of the printed text of the *Annals of Loch Cé*, eulogises him as the model of an Irish chief, but its praise of his military exploits and plundering expeditions hardly suggests a pious son of St Norbert. He was married to a daughter of the lord of Clanrickard, by whom he had a family. His son Brian certainly succeeded him in possession of the abbey, although I have not seen him referred to as abbot. One can also quote the comparable case of the last Maguire abbots of Lisgoole in Fermanagh, who held it for three generations down to 1603 by papal provision[6].

But if in the fifteenth and sixteenth centuries the monasteries had become completely secularised, it must not be supposed that the tradition of Christian asceticism and monastic piety was absent from Ireland. One of the most surprising facts, to our eyes, is the seeming inconsistency of its co-existence with the kind of monastic life which has been described above. Ascetic life in late medieval Ireland was in general confined to the friars and those under their influence, but an older ascetic tradition survived in the practice of anchoritism, which in Ireland went back to the early monastic tradition, though of course it was popular everywhere in Europe during the middle ages. The anchorite lived walled up in an apartment attached to a church, and such 'cells' existed at a number of churches in Ireland. Such examples were, however, of little importance compared with the enormous influence exercised by the friars, who alone in Gaelic Ireland attempted to maintain and preach the standards of European Christianity – though it is unlikely that they attempted, for example, to interfere with the native system of marriage and divorce. The writer of 1515 who has been quoted earlier declares that 'there is no . . . person of the church, high or low, great or small, English or Irish, that is accustomed to preach the word of God, saving the poor friars beggars.' The importance of their role is shown by the spread of their houses during the fifteenth and early sixteenth centuries. As was to be expected in a country where hardly any urban centres existed, the friaries in Gaelic and Gaelicised Ireland were mostly – contrary to the usual European pattern – rural; their distribution does not seem to follow any logical pattern, two or three – even of the same order – being sometimes found within a few miles while other areas possessed none at all. Most, though not all, owned some land – perhaps on average about a hundred acres – surrounding the house, and some Dominican and Carmelite houses had considerable landed property. Although the various orders of mendicant friars had established themselves soon after their foundation in the early thirteenth century, the early foundations were, as might be expected, of the usual urban type and most of the rural houses dated from the great expansion of the orders which accompanied the 'observant' movement (a movement aimed at restoring the original discipline of the mendicant orders, which had become modified in the course of time) in the fifteenth century. It must not be supposed that any current of hostility existed between the secularised church which has been described above and the friars; all the evidence, indeed, points the other way. Many of the members of the mendicant orders belonged to the old clerical families.

A noteworthy omission on the part of the Franciscans and Dominicans in medieval Ireland was their failure to introduce their corresponding orders of nuns. Houses of nuns were rare in Ireland and some of those which had existed in the thirteenth century had disappeared before the sixteenth; in 1431 the nunnery of St Catherine of Oconnell in County Limerick was dissolved by papal order as it possessed only one nun (who had married a layman and had children). Two noteworthy houses of nuns were Killone in Thomond and Kilcreevanty near Tuam, the abbesses of which were always chosen from the royal houses of O Brien and O Connor respectively.

Coarbs and erenaghs

The offices of coarb (*comharba*) and erenagh (*airchinneach*) are well known as survivals of an earlier stage of organisation in the late medieval Irish Church. It is however necessary to distinguish between the origins of these offices and their later functions, as well as between the two offices themselves. The coarb was literally the 'successor' of a saint, the founder of the Church; as the representative of the saint he was always to enjoy, down to the end, a considerable but undefinable spiritual prestige. The office had existed from early times, the coarb being of course originally the head of a monastic establishment which had been gradually secularised for the benefit of a particular family. The title of erenagh was of slightly later origin than that of coarb and originally also denoted the head of a monastic establishment, though he did not possess the spiritual prestige which attached to the coarbs as representative of the patron saint.

After the introduction of general European norms to the Irish Church the termons, the lands which belonged to the various native ecclesiastical establishments (most of which became parish churches under the new dispensation) were vested in the bishops. In Connacht we are explicitly told that this was carried out at a council held in 1210. In the completely Anglicised areas this resulted, with few exceptions, in the disappearance of the former occupiers, the coarbs and erenaghs and their clans, and the other quasi-ecclesiastical clans associated with these establishments; but in the Gaelic areas they remained in possession as tenants of the bishops, retaining their ecclesiastical status in so far as most of their members received minor orders and the greater part of the clergy proper continued to be drawn from their ranks. At the close of the sixteenth century it was stated that the erenaghs 'are accounted as clergymen and do most of them speak Latin, and they anciently used to have the tonsure [the first step to orders] but were always married.' The term erenagh came in the Gaelic areas to mean the head of a clan occupying Church lands under the bishop and a coarb was, therefore, simultaneously erenagh of the lands of his church. Thus in 1438 the bishop of Tír Bríuin appointed Nicholas O Farrelly as coarb of the church of St Maedhog of Drumlane and chief erenagh of the lands of his nation there. The erenagh, like an Irish chief or *ceann fine*, was the 'eldest and worthiest' of his clan, elected by the members and presented to the bishop for confirmation. If the bishop considered the erenagh-designate as unfit for the office, he could refuse to confirm him and force the clan to elect another, and if they failed to do so he could himself nominate one of their number as erenagh. If the clan in which the erenaghy was vested became extinct, the bishop could not keep the lands in his own hands but must instal a new erenagh family; this is no doubt the explanation of how the descendants of Ross Maguire, bishop of Clogher (1447–83), were in 1607 the erenaghs of Aghalurcher, or how the Mac Brady family occupied a large number of distinct erenaghys in the diocese of Kilmore.

Out of the Church lands which they held the erenaghs paid to the bishop a very low fixed rent, but they were also bound to furnish him with 'noxials' or refections, corresponding to the secular cuddy (see Chapter II), the value of which might amount to many times (thirty or forty times, according to Bishop Montgomery of Derry in 1607, but he may have exaggerated) the annual rent. These 'noxials' consisted of a night's lodging and entertainment for the bishop and his train once, twice, or four times in the year; like a secular lord, if the bishop did not wish to take them in person he might receive a payment in money or provisions instead. The erenaghs were also bound to provide the bishop with an 'aid' when he might request this for some special purpose, for, as the Coarb Dermot O Cahan said in 1607 of the relationship between the bishop and his tenants, 'all that we have belongs to the bishop, and we belong to him also', a statement which places the erenaghs – *nativi* of their bishop – on a par with the *nativi* of the bishop of Cloyne (also descendants of the old ecclesiastical families) in the fourteenth century. We find the descendants of some of these latter as 'freeholders' under the bishop in the sixteenth century. As well as their payments to the bishop the erenaghs – like, indeed, the beneficed Irish clergy in general – were bound to maintain hospitality for 'pilgrims, strangers and poor travellers.'

6   Economic Life

Agriculture and pastoralism

No other aspect of medieval Irish life and society is more scantily served by the surviving evidence than the economic basis of society, the cultivation of the land. Only the fact that linen cloth was one of the staple exports of late medieval Ireland, for instance, tells us, that flax cultivation must have been carried on on a considerable scale; there are no direct references. Of recent years the analysis of pollen deposits, although still at the initial stages, has thrown some light on agricultural matters, showing, for example, that – contrary to general belief – wheat was being cultivated in Tyrone through most of the later middle ages. There has certainly been a tendency to underestimate the importance of agriculture and correspondingly overestimate that of pastoralism in the Irish economy of the later middle ages; but this conclusion itself is probably derived from the conditions of the sixteenth century, when cultivation declined owing to the increasing violence and disturbance of the period. In times of trouble not only were cattle much less vulnerable than crops – they could be driven off into the woods or a neighbouring area, while crops and granaries had to be left at the mercy of an invader – but fighting men, while disdaining to stoop to manual toil, would not be unwilling to act as herdsmen. This, no doubt, is what is meant by a statement in the 1560s that the lords on the borders of the Pale were deliberately replacing cultivation by grazing in order 'to maintain their idle men of war'.

The staple grain crop of Ireland, owing to climatic factors, was oats, from which, with butter, were made the cakes – baked on an iron 'griddle' – which were the staple diet of the poorer Irish down to the introduction of the potato. Wheat was grown on a small scale in most parts of the country – more especially, if one may make a deduction from later practice, in the south-east – while in the Pale it was the staple food crop; the *Annals of Ulster* in their notice of the famine of 1497 record the price of wheat in Meath and of oats 'among the Gaels'. Barley was probably little grown outside the Pale, as it was the Irish custom to make ale from oat-malt, and the same would probably also have applied to rye. As regards methods of cultivation there must have been a wide difference between the unenclosed fields of the plains (see Chapter I) and the small plots found in the mountainous areas. The latter must have been cultivated, as they were down to modern times, with the spade, while the open fields were ploughed. From the end of the fourteenth century at least, the Irish plough-team was made up of horses, not oxen; eight 'garrans' (working-horses) made up a team, although as seventeenth-century observers always seem to refer to the plough as drawn by four horses we may wonder whether the eight-horse team does not represent two teams which drew two ploughs working in unison. This, however, is speculation. The size of the plough-team made it necessary for the poor to pool their horses for this purpose, and in fact there seems to have been a legal rule that tenants within the same townland were bound to do so if required. It was the custom to harness the horses to the plough by their tails, a practice revolting to English ideas and consequently – like the other Irish practice of burning the straw and chaff to leave the grain (which was said to thus have a pleasant taste) instead of threshing – forbidden by statute in the seventeenth century. (The idea behind ploughing by the tail was of course to cause the horses to stop if they should strike a rock or stump, instead of continuing with consequent damage to the plough or tackle.)

The normal kind of agricultural tenancy, at least in the sixteenth century, was a form of metayage, the tenant, if he provided his own stock and seed, paying the landlord a fourth of the crop ('the fourth sheaf'). The tenants to whom this applied would have been persons of some standing, possessing their own stock and so able to contract with their landlord on equal terms, and often his equals in wealth and position. In the Gaelic areas, however, much of the land seems to have been cultivated by the landowners or landowning clans themselves with the aid of labourers, who were probably remunerated with a share of the crop. Sir Rory O Shaughnessy (died 1569), lord of Kinelea in County Galway, is said once to have had two hundred reapers employed at his harvest. To this class of labourer rather than tenant would have belonged Maguire's 'own churls', with whom he cultivated his demesne lands around Enniskillen. In the English parts of the county of Wexford in 1610, the 'ancient custom' was that the landlord should provide half the seed and receive half the crop, the tenants being bound to provide all the labour of cultivation and to reap, bind, rick, thresh and cart the landlord's share. Before the division of the crop, however, the wages of those employed as reapers (who received two sheaves for a day's work) and the customary portion of the parish smith were deducted. In County Kilkenny and some similar areas a little earlier, we hear of tenants paying the 'third sheaf' as rent. Tenants everywhere were bound to follow the customary rotation of crops and fallow.

Although the amount of cultivation has certainly been underestimated, the importance of pastoralism in the medieval Irish economy cannot be overstressed. The Irish chiefs and notables possessed enormous numbers of cattle; in 1601 the son, grandson and cousin of Turlough Luineach O Neill each possessed two thousand head. Like some other pastoralists, the Irish no doubt tended on occasion to overstock their pastures, and certainly the pressure of stock must have been one of the most important causes of the destruction of the natural woodlands. The Irish cattle were small and usually black, apparently of the type nowadays represented by the Kerry breed. Milk products, such as butter, buttermilk and sour curds were of course part of the staple diet; like other pastoral peoples, such as the Tibetans and some African peoples, the Irish were also in the habit of drawing blood from the living cattle as a foodstuff, a practice which continued into the eighteenth century.

The herds and those in charge of them were collectively known as *caoruigheachta*, anglicised as kyrreaght and creaght (a word sometimes confused with creagh, *creach*, a cattle-raid, or 'prey'). The *caoruigheachta* are frequently mentioned in the historical sources, usually as fleeing or moving when their masters were exiled or returned from exile. The Ulster creaghts, as is well known, followed a more nomadic mode of existence than prevailed in the rest of the country; in a proclamation of the Lord Deputy in 1608 the inhabitants of Tyrone are said to pass the whole of the summer season moving from place to place with their herds, living in temporary shelters erected at each halting-place. But the custom of transferring the herds to summer pastures, usually in the mountains (transhumance or 'boolying'), was not peculiar to Ulster; it was general in all parts of Ireland during the period, the herds being accompanied by their herdsmen who lived for the summer in temporary dwellings on the pastures.

Besides providing foodstuffs, the herds were also the

IRELAND in 15th·16th Century
Centres of foreign trade

Principal trading towns ●
Fishing stations — Aran ⬡
Ports without urban development ( )

(Rafran and Moy Estuary
Killybegs
(Assaroe)
Lough Foyle)
The Bann
Carrickfergus
Ardglass
Sligo
Dundalk
Kells
Drogheda
Athboy
Navan
Mullingar
Trim
Dublin
Naas
Galway
Athenry
Wicklow
Arklow
Limerick
Kilkenny
Cashel
Callan
Fethard
New Ross
Clonmel
Wexford
Kilmallock
Carrick on Suir
Waterford
Dingle
Dungarvan
Fethard on Sea
Hook Head
Cork
Youghal
Dunmore East
Kinsale
Rosscarbery
(Berehaven)
Baltimore

0   80 Km
0   50 Mls

118

source of Ireland's most important export commodity, hides. Because of their commercial value, lords sometimes claimed a monopoly of hides within their territories; O Malley claimed in right of his chieftaincy to be entitled to the hides of all cattle slaughtered within his country.

Sheep and pigs were also kept on some scale, and at the end of the period we hear of herds of goats. The wool of the Irish sheep is described as being of coarse quality; it was used for the manufacture of friezes and rugs rather than of finer cloth. Lords and other persons of importance kept large herds of mares for the purposes of horse-breeding.

Foreign trade and the coastal towns

The materials for a history of the foreign trade of Ireland in the fifteenth and sixteenth centuries exist in the archives of many English and continental ports, but the history itself remains to be written. Although foreign trading vessels put into smaller havens – such as Ballyshannon or the Moy estuary – along the southern and western coasts, trade was almost entirely in the hands of the merchants of the independent corporate towns – Wexford, Ross, Waterford, Dungarvan, Youghal, Cork and Kinsale along the south coast, Dingle, Limerick, Galway and Sligo on the west, and Carrickfergus in the north. Curiously enough, until late in the sixteenth century and even later, the Irish merchants seem not to have gone in for ship-owning on any scale, preferring to charter ships from English or continental owners. The staple imports of the Irish trade were wine – of which enormous quantities were shipped from Bordeaux and the north Spanish ports to satisfy the taste of the upper classes – and salt; the staple exports hides, linen, and coarse woollens such as rugs and friezes. There must have existed a considerable linen industry to satisfy the needs of the foreign trade as well as domestic consumption, but we know nothing

119

of its organisation, or how the cloth was collected, for example, from the actual weavers.

The fisheries carried on off the southern and western coasts of Ireland were of great economic importance during the late medieval period, and brought in a large revenue to the lords of the adjacent coasts in the form of fishing-dues, charges for the use of harbours and of drying-grounds for nets and for the fish itself, etc. The fishery itself, however, was always carried on by foreign vessels, although Irish merchants might on occasion have a financial stake in it. In 1534 some merchants of Dingle contracted with a Breton sea-captain at Bordeaux to ship twenty tuns of wine – not a large quantity; in 1538 110 tuns were shipped from Bordeaux in a single ship by some Galway merchants – to Ireland; the cargo discharged, the vessel was to take on extra hands and engage in fishing off the Irish coast, returning to La Rochelle to dispose of her catch, the profits of which were to be divided between the merchants and the captain. The fisheries off Hook Head in the south-east, those centred on Baltimore in the south-west and the herring fishery off Aran Island in County Donegal are noted as being especially valuable.

The profits to be derived from foreign trade were very large, especially when compared with the relative poverty of Ireland in general. Their size was reflected in the pros-perity of the trading towns, which although small by European standards were well built and contained many fine houses. Luke Gernon, writing in 1620, describes the inner city of Limerick – the part situated on an island in the Shannon – as 'a lofty building of marble – in the High Street it is built from one gate to the other in the one form, like the colleges in Oxford, so magnificent that at my first entrance it did amaze me', and remarks also on the outer town on the south bank, 'fenced with such a huge strong wall that travellers affirm they have not seen the like in Europe' and on the magnificent quay, 200 yards long. The city of Cork he describes as being 'of stone and built after the Irish form, which is castle-wise and with narrow windows more for strength than for beauty.' Galway also, as can be seen from the famous pictorial map of 1650, was built in the same style. It is difficult to give an estimate of the population of any of these towns, as not only is there little information on which to base an estimate of the number of persons per dwelling but most of the labouring population would have lived in cabins outside the walls of which no record remains. Limerick in 1654 had over 400 houses within the walls and Waterford about the same number. Kilmallock in County Limerick had 260 houses and cabins, but some of the former were of large size. The number of freemen sharing in the municipal franchise and offices seems, however, to have been always low, as the control of affairs was restricted to a small group of aristocratic merchant families, the artisans and craftsmen being excluded. At the end of the period, in 1652, Galway had only 193 freemen, Cork only 253. The origins of these families were various, some representing old burgess families of the early period of English rule, others being local gentry families who had immigrated into the towns in the fifteenth century, either attracted by the profits of trade or to escape the oppressions of local lords. A surprising number of merchant families were, however, of Gaelic origin, such as the Ronaynes in Cork or the Kirwans and Dorseys in Galway. It is evident that while the merchant aristocracies constituted a highly select and entrenched élite they were not a closed caste, and it is reasonable to assume that their exclusiveness was directed rather against the artisan and craftsmen class, who would have constituted a possible threat to their control of municipal affairs, than against merchants of outside origin who could be absorbed into their own circle.

Patterns of settlement

Recent archaeological investigation has considerably modified the former belief that the Irish, before the Norman invasion, possessed no towns or nucleated settlements of any size, and has shown that considerable settlements of at least a quasi-urban nature existed around many of the important ecclesiastical centres, such as Clonard and Kildare. To the existence of such agglomerations of population may be ascribed the otherwise somewhat puzzling fact that a very large proportion, perhaps a majority, of the castles and motes erected by the Norman invaders were located at ecclesiastical sites, in spite of the difficulties with the Church to which this usually led. The majority of the Irish population before the invasion, however, certainly lived in isolated dwellings or in small groups of huts.

During the later middle ages broadly the same pattern was to persist in the purely Gaelic areas. Except possibly for the port of Sligo, there is no record of an Anglo-Norman borough continuing to exist under a Gaelic secular lord (Roscommon, for example, seems to have disappeared before the end of the fourteenth century) and the only known example of what could be called town development in a Gaelic lordship is Cavan, where some sort of town seems to have grown up under the O Reillys – a family whose lordship seems to have approximated more closely to a 'state' than most of its contemporaries – in the sixteenth century. The only urban centres in the purely Gaelic areas were the episcopal towns, such as Armagh and Rosscarbery (which in 1517 was a walled town containing 200 houses), while there may, as at an earlier date, have been also some nucleation around lesser ecclesiastical centres. In general, however, habitations must have been scattered or in small clusters. The insubstantial nature of most Irish dwellings, even those of persons of some standing, mere circular or ovoid huts of wattle and clay, without fireplaces and covered with thatch, militated against the formation of sizeable villages, as did, in the north, the custom of spending the summer wandering with the herds. In the areas of more intensive Norman settlement, where the process of Gaelicisation had never been complete, a tendency to a greater degree of nucleation seems to have survived. In the sixteenth century the episcopal towns mentioned above declined while in, for instance, Clanrickard the small boroughs of Loughrea and Clare-Galway, still existing around 1500, were in ruins by the middle of the century, a fate shared in the following years by the large and important trading town of Athenry.

PART II

HISTORICAL

IRELAND circa 1530
Showing principal lordships

Inishowen
ODOGHERTY

The Rout
MACQUILLIN

O CAHAN

MACDONNELLS

Tyrconnell
ODONNELL

O NEILL of
Clandeboy

Tyrone
ONEILL

SAVAGE

Lecale

Fermanagh
MAGUIRE

Iveagh
MAGENNIS

OHANLON

Tyrawley
BARRET

ODOWD

Sligo
O ROURKE

Oriel
MAC MAHON

Brefny

OREILLY

OHARA

OCONNOR

MACDONOGH

LOWER MAC WILLIAM

MAC JORDAN
MAC COSTELLO

MACDERMOT
THE TWO
O CONNORS

OMALLEY

MAC MORRIS

MAC DAVID
BURKE
BERMINGHAM

Annaly
O FARRELL

DALTON

Iarconnacht
OFLAHERTY

UPPER MAC WILLIAM

OKELLY

OMELAGHLIN
MAGEOGHAGAN

OMADDEN

OMOLLOY

EARL OF
KILDARE

Galway

Clanricard

Offaly
OCONNOR

Ormond Ely
OCARROLL

OKENNEDYS

OTOOLE

Arra
MACUIBRIAIN

Leix
OMORE

O BYRNE

Thomond
O BRIEN

MACGILLA
PATRICK

Kilkenny

MAC MURROUGH

OMULRIAN

Limerick

Clanwilliam
BURKES

BUTLERS

EARL OF DESMOND

Fermoy
ROCHE

POWER

Duhallow
MACDONOGH

FITZGERALD
of the Decies

BARRY MOR

Desmond
MACCARTHY MÔR Muskerry

OSULLIVAN
MÔR

Carbery
OSULLIVANBEARE MAC CARTHY REAGH

0   80 Km
0   50 Mls

126

7 Ulster

The O Neills of Tyrone

At the period of the Norman invasion of Ireland, as in later times, the most important native state of the north was that of the Cinéal Eóghain, which at that period stretched from the northern tip of Inishowen to the Blackwater near Armagh. In the late twelfth and early thirteenth centuries the kingship of the Cinéal Eóghain was being disputed between the families of Mac Loughlin – who had held it for most of the preceding century and a half – and O Neill. Hugh O Neill became king of Cinéal Eóghain in 1196 and retained power – save for a brief interval of Mac Loughlin rule in 1201 – until his death in 1230. He was an able and vigorous ruler who was not only able to resist the Norman attempts at penetration of his country but to twice interfere – in 1201 and 1226 – in the affairs of Connacht. On his death the kingship passed to Donnell Mac Loughlin who – after successfully disposing of two O Neill claimants who had temporarily dispossessed him, the second by English help – was in 1241 defeated and slain at Caimirghe (the place has not been located) by Brian O Neill, nephew of Hugh, in alliance with the O Donnells of Tirconnell. Ten of Donnell's clan who were eligible for the kingship of Cinéal Eóghain fell along with him at Caimirghe which, in striking contrast to the usual inconclusiveness of Irish warfare, was followed by the total disappearance of the Mac

Loughlins as a political force, the family surviving only as a minor clan in Inishowen.

The replacement of the Mac Loughlins by the O Neills led to a permanent shift in the location of power within Tyrone (Tír Eóghain), as we shall henceforth refer to it. For while the power of the Mac Loughlins seems to have been centred in the Strabane area, that of the O Neills was based in the south-east of Tyrone, in the region where in the fifteenth and sixteenth centuries their chief castle, Dungannon, was to be situated. This shift opened the way for the penetration of Inishowen and the north-west by their neighbours of Tirconnell, who had been interfering in these districts even in the twelfth century. In 1280, forty years after the fall of the Mac Loughlins, a Niall O Neill (whose identity is not quite certain) is described as king of Inishowen, but by 1300 most if not all of the peninsula was in the possession of the earl of Ulster, who had also – by rather dishonest means – secured possession of the city of Derry as the climax to a process of conquest and colonisation along the coastline of the present County Londonderry. After the death of the Brown Earl of Ulster in 1333 the Inishowen peninsula was taken over by a neighbouring chiefly family of Tirconnell, the O Dohertys, who became very numerous within the area, which they retained until the rebellion and death of Sir Cahir O Dogherty in 1608.

Brian O Neill, having put himself at the head of a great Gaelic confederacy to overthrow English rule in Ireland – of which he was chosen to be the future king – was defeated and slain at the battle of Down in 1260. His successor Hugh Buidhe – the eponym of the later Clann Aodha Buidhe, Clandeboy – was a man of very different politics, who married a cousin of the earl of Ulster and was retained in the service of the crown 'to keep peace in the marches of Ulster'. After his death Donnell son of Brian O Neill made himself king of Cinéal Eóghain, in spite of two attempts by the earl of Ulster to replace him by, in turn, the brother and son of Hugh Buidhe, both of whom were slain by Donnell. In 1307 the latter is found styling himself 'king of the Irish of Ulster', and in 1318, when he addressed the famous 'Remonstrance' to the pope on the wrongs of the Irish, 'king of Ulster'. Neither title had been previously used by the kings of Cinéal Eóghain, the name Ulster (Uladh) at the time of the invasion being used almost exclusively for the modern Counties Antrim and Down, then the kingdom of the Mac Dunlevys (see below). After Donnell's death in 1325 his son Hugh and Henry O Neill, grandson of Hugh Buidhe, ruled in opposition to each other until 1345, when the Justiciar Sir Ralph de Ufford deposed Henry, who then currently bore the title of king of Ulster, in favour of Hugh, a reversal of the usual English policy of supporting the Clann Aodha Buidhe

Niall Mór O Neill succeeded his father Hugh in 1364, but until 1379 had to contend with intermittent armed opposition from his brother Donnell. A great warrior, the long and successful campaigns which he waged against the colony in Ulster resulted in the virtual disappearance of the latter; it is ironical that the beneficiaries of his campaigns were not to be his descendants but the rival house of Clann Aodha Buidhe. The less desirable side of the Gaelic reconquest is displayed by the evidence which is to be found in the Armagh archiepiscopal registers on the oppressions and extortions committed at this period by the O Neills – especially the sons and grandsons of Niall Mór – on the city of Armagh and its clerical inhabitants. A curious picture of Niall Mór's court and army has been left by the Catalan knight Perelhos, who visited him in 1397, the year before his death, although to balance the picture of scarcity which Perelhos paints it is necessary to remember that 1397 was a year of crop-failure in Ireland. In 1395 Niall Mór had personally made submission to Richard II at Drogheda, promising to recognise the earl of March's claims as heir to the earldom of Ulster – although his life had been spent in effectively destroying its material basis. He was probably largely moved in submitting by concern for his grandsons, given as hostages to the English in exchange for his son Niall Óg who had been captured in 1389. Niall Óg was to succeed his father, but died in 1403. Another son, Henry Aimhréidh, had settled in the north-west of Tyrone, the district called Cinéal Moen, where he built the castle near Newtown-Stewart called in the fifteenth and sixteenth centuries – as the first of its kind in the area – 'the old castle' but today, after its founder, 'Harry Averay's Castle'. Its purpose was no doubt to consolidate the O Neill hold on the district, which during the fifteenth and sixteenth centuries, like the tribute and overlordship of Inishowen, was constantly in contention between the O Neills and O Donnells. A third son of Niall Mór, Cú-Ula, settled near Armagh, where his sons, notorious oppressors of the Church, dispossessed the archbishop and his clerical tenants of many lands which they and their descendants were to retain.

The rule of Donnell O Neill, Henry Aimhréidh's son and successor to his uncle Niall Óg, was largely occupied down to his death at the hands of the O Cahans in 1432, in a struggle with his cousin Owen, son of Niall Óg, in which each contender was more than once captured or exiled by the other. On Donnell's death Owen was inaugurated as O Neill on the Stone of the Kings at Tullaghoge. At this period there begins a feature which was to characterise the history of Tyrone during the following century and a half, the existence of a clan of O Neills permanently hostile to the ruling O Neill and allied with O Donnell in the north-west of Tyrone. The actual clan which played this role changed from time to time, but the principle remained the same. In succession the descendants of Henry Aimhréidh (Sliocht Henrí), those of Owen's son Art of Omagh, who died in 1458 (Sliocht Airt) and those of Art Óg O Neill (died 1519) filled this position. Owen's long and successful rule, marked by frequent raids on the Pale and by wars with the O Donnells, ended in 1455 when he resigned (or was deposed) in favour of his son Henry. Other sons of Owen were settled in various areas on the frontiers of Tyrone which passed to their descendants. Art had the district around Omagh; Hugh (died 1475), tanist to his brother Henry, held the district of the Fews to the north-west of Dundalk which his father had seized from the loyal Anglo-Norman Bellews (the O Neills, as part of their treaty with the duke of York in 1449, had promised to restore it but of course had not done so). The descendants of other sons, such as Murtough and Felim, occupied other areas.

From 1458, when his brother Art died, Henry O Neill was engaged in a struggle with Art's sons in which they were backed by O Donnell and which centred round the possession of the castle of Omagh. In 1483 Henry resigned in favour of his son Conn, who had married a sister of the Great Earl of Kildare. The latter was from this on to frequently interfere in the affairs of Tyrone. Conn was murdered in 1493 by his half-brother Henry Óg, who made himself O Neill with the support of the Sliocht Airt. He was continually opposed, though with little success, by another brother, Donnell, who became undisputed O Neill in 1498 when Henry Óg was slain in the house of his cousin, the lord of Fews, by Conn's sons by Kildare's sister. In attempting to take the castle of Dungannon from Henry Óg's faction, however, Donnell was severely defeated by the latter and it was not until the earl of Kildare had come into Tyrone with an army, taken Dungannon and compelled the submission of the Sliocht Airt that Donnell was securely established. His successor was his cousin Art, lord of Fews (whose descendants were to be lords of that district down to the seventeenth century), on whose death in 1513 Art Óg, son of Conn by his first wife (not Kildare's sister) became O Neill, again with the assistance of the earl of Kildare. Art's full-brother Shane (died 1517) became tanist to his brother; it is typical of Irish politics at the period that in 1516 he was to incite O Donnell to invade Tyrone because his brother had failed to support him in a quarrel with his kinsmen of Fews. He was the ancestor of the O Neills of Kinard (now Caledon), who occupied a prominent and quasi-independent position in the sixteenth century and to whom belonged Sir Felim O Neill, the leader of the 1641 rising in Ulster. On Art's death in 1519 his successor was his half-brother Conn Bacach, Kildare's cousin. Conn Bacach was a remarkably able and ambitious man, whose plans – such as his hope to force the O Donnells into acknowledging O Neill overlordship – outran his resources. In 1522, for example, he organised a great confederacy of both Ulster and Connacht against O Donnell, but on his own defeat by the latter it dissolved. In Tyrone itself he found a persistent opposition in the persons of his nephews, Niall Conallach and the other sons of Art Óg, who took the part of O Donnell. Conversely the Sliocht Airt – who had been constantly at war with Art Óg and whose territorial interests were directly threatened by his sons – took the part of O Neill. The struggle between Art Óg's sons and the Sliocht Airt, which eventually resulted in the dominance of the former in north-west Tyrone, was a ruthless one in which four of Art Óg's sons perished by hanging, two at the hands of the Sliocht Airt and two at those of their uncle Conn Bacach. The death of Niall himself in 1544 temporarily left Conn without opposition in this direction.

Conn Bacach submitted to Henry VIII in 1542 and was created earl of Tyrone, with remainder to his eldest surviving son Fardoragh – a mere 'named' son whom, it was alleged, had been believed to be a smith's son for the first sixteen years of his life – who himself became baron of Dungannon. By 1551 relations between the father and son were very bad and the latter was assisting the English against Conn. A younger son, Shane Donnghaileach, was however already rising to prominence; in 1558 he killed Fardoragh and on Conn's death in the following year became O Neill without opposition. His career belongs to the general history of the period; it may be remarked, however, that his ability and ruthlessness enabled him to realise his father's dream of subjugating the O Donnells. On his death Niall Conallach's son Turlough Luineach became O Neill and remained so until forced to abdicate in favour of Hugh, earl of Tyrone (a son of Fardoragh) in 1593. His sons Sir Art and Cormac successively played some part, as leaders of their sept, in the wars of Hugh O Neill's rebellion, but both were dead by 1603, leaving Hugh in a position of undisputed control in Tyrone, which lasted until his flight in 1607.

'Little Ulster' and Clandeboy

The former kingdom of Uladh, ruled before its conquest by John de Courcy by the Mac Dunlevys, became the only region of Ulster densely settled by the invaders. Apart from the western part of County Down – which will be mentioned below – and the district of Uí Tuirtre along the eastern bank of the lower Bann, the country was parcelled out into fiefs and tenancies and a string of boroughs founded, of which Coleraine and Portrush were the most northern. After the slaying of the Brown Earl of Ulster in 1333 the colony in Ulster remained for some time intact. Its greatest Anglo-Norman family the Mandevilles, however, disappeared soon after, leaving the Savages as the acknowledged leaders of the Ulster settlers. By 1350 the colony was being attacked by the

O Cahans, its neighbours across the Bann to the west, and the Mac Quillins, who had been hereditary captains of mercenaries under the earls of Ulster but were already in revolt. The Elizabethan legend that the family of Mac Quillin (Mac Houlyn, *Mac Uighilin*) descended from the Mandevilles, though often repeated, is on a par with similar legends which made FitzUrses out of the Mac Mahons and the Mortimers out of the Mac Namaras; they probably came originally from the south-west of Scotland. Stephen Mac Quillin had been appointed constable to the earl of Ulster, an office formerly held by his father, in 1331; by 1351 he was, as we have seen, being classed as a rebel and with Hugh O Neill of Tyrone and Mac Mahon of Oriel was the target of an expedition by the justiciar, Sir Thomas de Rokeby, of which little is known. He died in 1368, still styled constable of Ulster. The name of the mercenary force led by the Mac Quillins – 'the Rout of Mac Quillin' – became transferred to their territory in the north of County Antrim, formerly known as Tuaisceart and centred on the castle of Dunluce (a former possession of the Mandevilles), where the family remained powerful throughout the fifteenth and early sixteenth centuries. After about 1550 they suddenly and inexplicably declined; by the 1570s almost all of the Rout was in the hands of the Mac Donnells.

We know strangely little of the details of the destruction of the Ulster colony and the rise of Clandeboy. The accounts of the earldom in 1350 and 1351 show the boroughs and demesne manors still flourishing, although there was some disturbance in the countryside. The actual destruction seems to have been largely the work of Niall Mór O Neill, and it is ironical that the actual beneficiaries were not his descendants but their rivals and enemies of the Clann Aodha Buidhe (Clandeboy). The latter, from their original settlement in the south-east of County Londonderry (Glanconkeen), seem to have moved across the Bann and dispossessed the Gaelic O Flinns of Uí Tuirtre around or soon after 1350. A Scottish tradition ascribes their rise to assistance from the Mac Donnell lords of the Isles to whom they were related by marriage, and in 1404 the Irish annals record that the whole colony was wasted, the English driven out and Downpatrick, Coleraine and the abbey of Inch burned by a coalition of Scotsmen with Magennis (see below) and Mac Gillamurry, a local Irish chief. There is no mention in this of the contemporary head of the Clandeboy, Brian Ballach, who fell at the hands of the burghers of Carrickfergus in 1426 and who was probably the consolidator of the clan's dominion in the area. From about 1431 the seneschalsy of the earldom of Ulster, at this time restricted to a small area in County Down, passed between the Savages – who from this time on were restricted to the peninsula of Ards – and their less Gaelicised neighbours, the Whites of Dufferin. In 1481 Patrick Óg Savage, seneschal of Ulster, was captured, blinded and castrated by Conn O Neill of Clandeboy who had slain Patrick's brother and predecessor in 1468. His successor Rowland Savage had before his death in 1519 been driven from his country, with the other Anglo-Normans of Lecale, by Glaisne Magennis, abbot of Newry and prior of Down, who was supported by the earl of Kildare. After the prior's death the Savages (who were by this time completely Gaelicised) returned, but the Whites disappeared for a time from the Ulster scene, retiring to live in the Pale and leaving Dufferin to be occupied until the 1550s by Mac Donnell immigrants from Scotland.

As enemies to the O Neills of Tyrone the O Neills of Clandeboy were traditional allies of the O Donnells. Their power continued to increase down to the death of Hugh Meirgeach O Neill in a battle with the earl of Kildare's forces in 1525, but after the death of Niall Óg in 1537 no single lord succeeded in gaining control and by the 1560s Clandeboy was divided into northern and southern sections. The political scene in Clandeboy and the Rout at this period is one of such extreme confusion and dispersion as to suggest that the political institutions and divisions of the country had never acquired any great degree of stability.

Before 1400 the district known as the Glens – the coastal region of north-eastern Antrim – had come by marriage into the hands of John Mór Mac Donnell, a son of the lord of the Isles, whose descendants were to retain it. As they were also lords of Kintyre and Islay, their interests tended to be in Scotland rather than in Ireland until the sixteenth century. In the second half of the sixteenth century the famous Sorley Buidhe Mac Donnell succeeded in annexing most of the Rout of Mac Quillin; his lands passed intact to his sons, of whom the younger was eventually created earl of Antrim.

The western part of County Down, corresponding to the diocese of Dromore, had been the kingdom of Dál Araidhe. In later times it was known, from its ruling stock (the Uí Eachach) as Iveagh. Perhaps owing to the wooded nature of the country, it was almost unaffected by Anglo-Norman penetration, although its kings – belonging to the families of O Haddy and Mac Cartan – paid tribute, like the other Irish lords of Ulster, to the earls of Ulster. After the capture and execution of Thomas Mac Cartan, king of Iveagh, by the English in 1347 the headship passed to another family of the area, the Magennises. Little is known of their history before the sixteenth century, in which they figure prominently.

Tirconnell

The O Donnells of Tirconnell are among the most famous of Irish ruling families. Their fame is at least partly due to their possessing able and partisan chroniclers – indeed sometimes panegyrists – in the annalists of Donegal, the *Four Masters*, but certainly the family in the fifteenth and sixteenth centuries consistently showed a hardness and sense of political purpose absent from most Irish rulers.

At the end of the twelfth century the O Donnells were one of a number of clans disputing the kingship of the Cinéal Conaill – of Tirconnell – and it is not until after the death of Niall O Cananain in 1250 that we find an uninterrupted O Donnell succession. The latter half of the thirteenth century saw the settlement in Tirconnell of the Scots-Norse Mac Sweenys, who dispossessed many of the old chieftain families and became the most important vassals of the O Donnells. After the murder of Connor O Donnell by his brother Niall in 1342 a period of disturbance followed, and the struggles over the chieftaincy were not finally resolved until Connor's son Shane O Donnell was slain in battle by Niall's son Turlough in 1380. During this period Shane O Donnell had been defeated in 1359 by Cahal Óg Ó Connor of Sligo, who had thereafter ruled Tirconnell for a short time. With Turlough (*'an fhiona'*, 'of the wine') began the period of O Donnell prominence, during which they began to interfere in the affairs of Connacht. Turlough's son Niall Garve was captured by the English while raiding the Pale in company with O Neill in 1434, and died a prisoner in the Isle of Man in 1439. His place was taken by his brother Naghten, who was slain by Niall Garve's sons in 1452. A struggle ensued until Hugh Roe, son of Niall, captured and mutilated the then lord, Turlough Cairbreach son of Naghten, in 1461 and became undisputed O Donnell, although in 1480 he was forced to recognise another son of Naghten as tanist. In 1497 the tanist was slain by Hugh Roe's son Conn, in whose favour his father then abdicated, only to resume his lordship when Conn was slain in battle by O Neill a few months later. On his death in 1505 Hugh Roe was succeeded by his son Hugh Duff, and he in 1537 by his son Manus.

Throughout the fifteenth and sixteenth centuries, a continual cause of dispute existed between the O Donnells and O Neills over the tribute of Inishowen and the possession of the area known as Cinéal Moen, on the borders of the present counties of Tyrone and Donegal. The present county boundary represents the eventual *de facto* division of the latter area between the contenders. Under the two Hughs, father and son, the O Donnells found a more fruitful field for expansion in the south. Fermanagh and the northern parts of Connacht were laid under permanent tribute, and the latter unfortunate province came to be the victim of almost yearly creaghs by the O Donnells. These encroachments were favoured by the fact that after 1500 both the Maguireship and the Lower Mac Williamship passed through periods of weakness which made their countries in no real position to resist aggression. An attempt by Conn Bacach O Neill to repress the O Donnells by means of a general confederacy of Ulster and Connacht lords in 1522 ended in disaster. The political-mindedness of the O Donnells is shown by the relations which they cultivated at this period with the court of Scotland. In 1555 Manus O Donnell was attacked and taken prisoner by his own son Calvagh, who thereupon assumed the lordship, keeping his father in prison until the latter's death in 1564. The subsequent wars between Calvagh and his brothers – who were assisted by Shane O Neill – as well as the bringing of Connacht under English control, with a consequent end to O Donnell tribute from that province, greatly weakened the O Donnell power, but Tirconnell in fact remained autonomous and beyond any effective internal interference by the central government, until 1603. Calvagh's successor (in 1566) was his half-brother Hugh, who ruled until he abdicated in favour of his son, the famous Hugh Ruadh, in 1592.

During the thirteenth century members of various families are occasionally named as kings of Fermanagh, but it seems probable that the country was often disunited. The first Maguire to become lord of all Fermanagh, in or around 1282, was Donn, the founder of a dynasty which was to enjoy what was, by Irish standards, remarkable stability and freedom from internal dissension down to 1484. In 1484 Gillapatrick Maguire, son and tanist to the then ruler Edmond, was murdered at the altar of Agha-lurgher church by his own half-brothers, and a civil war broke out, resolved in 1486 by Edmond's abdication in favour of a cousin, Shane mac Philip Maguire of Ennis-killen. On Shane's death in 1504 a period of weakness ensued, during which the country came under the suzerainty of the O Donnells, who occupied some western districts. In 1542 these districts were returned by Manus O Donnell to another Shane Maguire – who had been placed in the lordship by Conn Bacach O Neill in 1540 – on condition that Maguire entered into onerous tribute relations and agreed to furnish O Donnell with the 'rising-out' of the country (see Chapter IV) when required. Shane was the first Maguire to enter into direct relations with the English government in Ireland. On his death in 1566 he was succeeded by his brother Cúchonnacht Óg, who ruled until 1589.

The Mac Mahons of Oriel, unlike the Maguires, were not a new ruling family which first appears in the thirteenth century but represented a branch of the old royal house of O Carroll which had adopted a new surname. Anglo-Norman colonisation in the region, the modern County Monaghan, had never penetrated – apart from the build-ing of a castle, destroyed next year by O Neill, at Clones in 1212 – beyond the baronies of Farney and Cremorne, and by 1280 Ralph Pippard, the nominal lord of the region, was leasing Cremorne to a Mac Mahon on fairly easy terms. The contemporary Mac Mahon was Brian, 'king of Oriel', who in 1297, with his brother and his other vassals, entered into a remarkable treaty with the bishop of Clogher which shows them to have been in effective control of almost the whole of the modern county. During the late fourteenth and the fifteenth centuries a succession of able rulers strengthened and consolidated their position, levying blackmail from the English of Louth with whom they were frequently at war. Nevertheless, the lordship of Farney was usually leased by the crown to a Mac Mahon until, in the second half of the fifteenth century, it fell permanently into the hands of the latter, who penetrated even further to occupy Stonetown, County Louth, which remained in their possession until 1581. The usual internal dissensions broke out over the succession in the later fifteenth century, and after the accession of Redmond (II) in 1513 the lordships of Dartry and Farney, ruled by other branches of the family, were practically independent of the Mac Mahonship. Hugh Ruadh Mac Mahon, who had suc-ceeded his brother Sir Ross Buidhe in 1589, fell a victim to the Lord Deputy Sir William Fitzwilliam, who had him tried and executed on a trumped-up charge in 1592. This was followed by a settlement of County Monaghan in which no one chief was recognised but the county – except for Farney, which had been granted to the earl of Essex in 1575, although he seems never to have got possession – was divided among several of the principal men of the family, under whom only a selected – but still large – number of the lesser freeholders received lands.

8   Connacht

The O Connors down to the Bruce invasion

The history of the kingship of Connacht during most of the thirteenth century belongs rather to the general history of Ireland as a whole. Although William de Burgo had obtained a speculative grant of Connacht from John around 1195, his death in 1203 put an end for the time being to encroachments on the province west of the Shannon, and Cahal Crobhdearg O Connor was able to preserve the integrity of his kingdom until his death in 1224. Cahal's son and successor Hugh was driven from his kingdom by his cousins, the sons of the former high-king Rory O Connor, with the support of most of the Connacht lords, and although he succeeded in re-establishing himself with the aid of the Justiciar, the earl Marshal, King Henry III had meanwhile been persuaded to make a new grant of Connacht to Richard de Burgo, William's son. The latter, in alliance with the sons of Rory, invaded Connacht and expelled Hugh, who was murdered (for private reasons) by an Englishman soon after. There followed a period of long-drawn out wars in which the province was devastated in a three-cornered struggle between de Burgo, the sons of Rory and Hugh's brother Felim. Finally, after 1235, a *modus vivendi* was reached by which Felim O Connor was left in possession of the 'five cantreds' which had been reserved by the King in his grant to de Burgo, while the remainder of the province was parcelled out by the latter among his barons and knights. Although socially the colonisation of Connacht would appear to have been rather superficial, politically it was sufficiently strong for the death of Richard de Burgo ten years later and the minority of his heir to make no difference to the situation. In 1249 King Felim was dragged into a war with the English by his son Hugh – who was to show a consistent hostility to the settlers during his life – which led to Felim's temporary deposition and banishment by the justiciar, Maurice Fitz Gerald, in favour of his nephew Turlough mac Hugh. He returned, however, in the following year and was again recognised by the government. From this time onwards, however, King Henry began to make grants to his favourites in the southernmost part of the 'five cantreds', Omany (Uí Maine) and Tirmany. On King Felim's death in 1265 he was succeeded by his son Hugh, who throughout his reign was involved in continuous and more or less successful war against Walter de Burgo, earl of Ulster and lord of Connacht – whom he defeated in 1268 and again, at Athanchip, in 1270 – and with the government. In 1269 the Justiciar, Robert d'Ufford, built a castle at Roscommon in the heart of O Connor territory, but in 1272 it was destroyed by Hugh along with the town of Athlone. His enemy Walter de Burgo had died in 1271, leaving a minor heir, but Hugh's own death in 1274 left the O Connor kingship in chaos. His immediate successors were ephemeral and with little authority over their own 'iraghts'.

After the death of Hugh mac Felim the southern half of the 'five cantreds', extending north to Roscommon and Ballintober – where two strong castles were erected – was taken into the hands of the crown and was for the most part parcelled out among Anglo-Norman grantees and fee-farm tenants. Only the northernmost part, the cantred of 'Tothes' (Trí tuatha) in north-eastern Roscommon, Moylurg and Tirerrill, remained in the hands of the O Connors and their 'iraghts', of whom the most important were the Mac Dermots of Moylurg. The Mac Dermot power was centred on the strong island fortress of the Rock of Lough Key, which plays a prominent part in the history of the area at this period and later. A branch of the Mac Dermots were the Mac Donoghs, descendants of a Donogh who died in 1232, who in the person of Donogh's grandson Tomaltagh (died 1333) became lords of Tirerrill. During the forty years which followed the death of Hugh mac Felim the kingship of Connacht, restricted to this narrow extent, was disputed between the descendants of Hugh mac Cahal Cróbhdearg and the Clan Murtough, the descendants of Cahal's brother Murtough Muimhneach.

When Edward Bruce's invasion of Ireland took place in 1315 the then king of Connacht, Felim O Connor, a very young man who had been made king by his foster-father Mac Dermot in 1310, joined the Red Earl of Ulster to resist Bruce. He was, however, not immune to advances by the latter offering him the sovereignty of all Connacht, but before he could make any response the initiative in this direction was seized by a rival, Rory O Connor of the Clan Murtough, who made himself king. After bitter and destructive fighting, Rory was defeated and slain by Felim, with the help of Richard de Bermingham of Athenry, in February, 1316. Felim then turned against the Anglo-Norman lords of Connacht, against whom he gained some success, but in August he was defeated and slain at Athenry, with most of his principal vassals and allies, by an army led by Richard de Bermingham and the earl's cousin, Sir William Liath de Burgo.

The rise of the Mac Williamships and the wars of faction
It is a demonstration of the utter destruction of the basis of English power in Ireland wrought by the Bruce invasion

that the battle of Athenry – remembered long after in the Pale as a great English victory over the Gaelic Irish, although both the victorious commanders were the husbands of Gaelic Irishwomen and their descendants were to be completely Gaelicised within a couple of generations – should have been followed by an immediate resurgence of Gaelic power in Connacht. Aughrim, the head of the Butler lordship of Omany, had been burned by the O Kellys, its native Gaelic lords, in 1316 and there is no evidence that the Butlers ever returned to it. In 1397 the then O Kelly was claiming that his family had occupied the former Butler lands for eighty years, which would place their recovery by the O Kellys immediately after 1316. Although the borough of Roscommon was to survive for another forty-five years at least, the rural English landowners in its neighbourhood disappear, with the exception of the powerful Sir David de Burgo, whose descendants, the Mac Davids of Clanconway (Clann Conmhaigh), were to hold their lands in the heart of the O Connor territory down to the seventeenth century.

In 1317 Turlough O Connor, a brother of the dead king Felim, was made king of Connacht in place of a kinsman. In March, 1318, he had a grant from the crown of the lands of Silmurray (the O Connor homeland around Roscommon and Ballintober), Tirmany (southern County Roscommon) and the Faes (the district adjoining Athlone) to hold at the usual rents, but later in the same year he was deposed by Cahal O Connor, head of another clan of O Connors, the Clan Aindriais, who were settled in the neighbourhood of Sligo. In 1324 Cahal was slain by Turlough, who thereupon resumed the kingship, but within a few years he was to be threatened by a rival of another kind. Walter Mac William de Burgo, William Liath's son, had probably succeeded his father as the Red Earl's representative in Connacht; the death of the earl in 1326 left him in a virtually independent position there.

Both English and Irish sources agree that he had ambitions to make himself independent king of Connacht. The subsequent fighting between Mac William and Turlough O Connor, who was supported by the young earl of Ulster and his uncle, Sir Edmond, the Red Earl's son, led to the defeat of Mac William, who was captured (1332) by the earl and starved to death as a prisoner in the castle of Northburgh in Inishowen. In the following year, and to avenge his death, the earl was himself assassinated by some of the English of Ulster.

The death of the Brown Earl of Ulster, who left only a minor daughter and heir, saw his ally Turlough O Connor in a far stronger territorial position than any king of Connacht had occupied since the time of Felim, son of Cahal Crobhdearg, or even his predecessor Hugh. The only real bar to the expansion of his power was the rise of the O Kellys, who had been incited by Walter de Burgo to resist him on his southern frontier in Tirmany and the Faes. The administration of the de Burgo lordship was meanwhile confided by the crown to Sir Edmond, the Red Earl's son, who was supported by Richard 'le Hore' de Burgo, the head of a branch of the family known as the Clann Ricaird (Clanrickard, *Ricardini*) and by Thomas de Bermingham of Athenry. In 1335 they were the targets of a massive attack led by another Sir Edmond de Burgo, Edmond Albanach ('the Scot'), brother of the deceased Mac William, whose position in Connacht politics he had assumed. In 1338 Sir Edmond Albanach succeeded in capturing his namesake and – doubtless in revenge for the part he had played in the death of Walter – drowned him in Lough Mask. The role of avenger of his death was taken over by Turlough O Connor, who married the dead man's widow – his own maternal aunt – and succeeded in driving Sir Edmond out of Connacht. The latter conducted a naval war for some time, but in 1340 he and his brother secured a pardon from the crown and seem to have been able to re-establish themselves in Connacht. In 1342 Turlough O Connor, having fallen out with Mac Dermot, was deposed by the latter and by Sir Edmond Albanach (two of whose near kinsmen had been murdered at Turlough's instigation) and Hugh O Connor of the Clan Murtough was made king. His rule did not however, last, and Turlough remained king until his death in a skirmish in 1345, when he was succeeded by his son Hugh. The latter fell victim to a private revenge in 1356, when his cousin Hugh mac Felim, the ally and protégé of Sir Edmond Albanach, who had previously succeeded in making him a king for a year in 1350–51, became king without opposition.

During this period continual warfare raged between Sir Edmond Albanach, his kinsfolk and supporters on one hand and the Clanrickard on the other. The pattern of alliances which came into existence at this date was to persist throughout the whole medieval history of Connacht: even in the late sixteenth century the political allegiances centred on the two great factions, those headed by the Lower and Upper (Clanrickard) Mac Williams respectively, were still a living thing. The same period also saw the disappearance of the authority of the crown in Connacht; in 1347 the justiciar Sir Walter de Bermingham had obtained the submission of the Anglo-Norman lords of Connacht, including Sir Edmond and his enemies of Clanrickard, who had given hostages, but thereafter all control ceases. In 1358 it was recorded that the rents of the earl of Ulster's heir in Connacht could not be collected because of the war between Sir Edmond de Burgo and the 'Ricardines'; an attempt two years later to recover them produced only 18s 4d, of which meagre sum – along with his own clothes and possessions – the collector, who had not felt able to afford an escort, was robbed on his way back by the Irish of Ormond. The royal castles of Rindown and

Roscommon seem to have fallen into the hands of the Irish some time in the 1350s; the borough of Roscommon, which had endured for forty years as an English urban island in a Gaelic sea, disappears from view with the record of its burning in 1360. The demesne manors of the earls of Ulster were taken over either by the neighbouring Irish – as Sligo and Ballymote – or by the junior de Burgos – as Loughrea – by the Clanrickard. Meelick and its cantred of Síl Anmchadha are a special case; they had been granted for life by the Red Earl to the native Gaelic lord, Owen O Madden, in reward for the latter's loyalty, alone among the Irish of Connacht, throughout the Bruce wars, and were retained by O Madden's descendants. None of the resident Anglo-Norman lords would appear to have suffered seriously through the Gaelic revival except the de Berminghams, whose scattered lands were particularly vulnerable; not only had the O Dowdas extinguished their interests in Tireragh by the early fifteenth century but their territories around Athenry had fallen victim to serious encroachment by the O Kellys, whose expansion is one of the most notable features of the late fourteenth century in Connacht.

Hugh mac Felim O Connor was succeeded as king of Connacht by Rory son of Turlough, an able man who maintained the high prestige and power which the O Connor kingship had succeeded in re-acquiring. In 1377 he defeated the new Mac William, Edmond Albanach's son Sir Thomas (who had succeeded his father in 1375) in a pitched battle at Roscommon. On Rory's death in 1384, however, the fatal division of the O Connors began, two rival kings being proclaimed: Turlough Ruadh (Roe), son of Hugh mac Felim and Turlough Óg, son of Hugh mac Turlough, the former being supported by Sir Thomas and the latter being supported by the Clanrickard, by Mac Donogh and by the O Connors of Sligo. A long war then began in which neither side succeeded in gaining any lasting advantage. On the death of Turlough Óg, murdered by the Mac David Burkes in 1406, his cousin Cahal mac Rory was proclaimed king in opposition to Turlough Ruadh. Although Cahal was captured by his enemies in the next year and remained a prisoner until he was exchanged in 1420 for O Kelly, recently captured in a great defeat which the *Ruadh* faction suffered at the hands of Clanrickard and the O Briens in their invasion of Clanrickard, his supporters held out and defended the castle of Roscommon against an almost continuous siege by their opponents. William O Kelly, tanist of Uí Maine, played the leading role in the latter part of this siege, probably – judging by the encroachments which the O Kellys made on the O Connors in this area – motivated more by the hope of retaining it himself than of delivering it to Turlough Ruadh. After the latter's death in 1426 Cahal was recognised as sole king until his death in 1439, but the power of the O Connors, revived under King Turlough and his successors, was now decisively broken and after Cahal's death they were permanently divided into the lines of Donn and Ruadh (Roe) and rapidly sank into insignificance. The title of king of Connacht disappears after the 1460s.

The later period

During the fifteenth century the two major powers in Connacht were the two Mac Williams, with Mac Dermot and O Connor of Sligo in perhaps the second place. During the last quarter of the fourteenth century Sir Thomas de Burgo, Edmond Albanach's son, and his rival Sir William or Ulick (who had succeeded his father Richard Óg as lord of Clanrickard in 1382) had alternated as the official representatives of the Dublin government in Connacht, according as each possessed the ear of different adminstrations. But after Sir Thomas's death in 1401 his line lost all contact with the Dublin adminstration, while the Clanrickards continued to hold a shadowy sheriffdom of Connacht through the century. Until the close of the century the Lower (i.e. northern) Mac Williams, Sir Edmond Albanach's descendants, were probably on balance the stronger, but their power then suffered a severe decline owing to a number of different factors, such as internal disputes and changes in the internal politics of the Mac Dermots of Moylurg which led after 1497 to the replacement of a line allied with the Lower Mac Williams by one favourable to the Upper (i.e. southern, Clanrickard). Most important of all, however, was their break with their former allies the O Donnells owing to the increasing power of the latter, which had led them to interfere more and more in the affairs of Sligo and of Lower (northern) Connacht in general. Connacht resistance to O Donnell was seldom effectual, and when in 1522 Conn Bacach O Neill succeeded in organising a confederacy under Mac William of Clanrickard which would co-operate in a double attack on Tirconnell, the enterprise ended in humiliating failure.

Clanrickard seems to have been free from succession disputes down to 1536, and the power of its lords suffered only a temporary check by the defeat of Ulick Finn (1485–1509) by the earl of Kildare at Knockdoe in 1504. A succession dispute after 1536 was resolved by the intervention of the Lord Deputy, Lord Leonard Grey, who deposed both contenders in favour of a third candidate, Ulick na gCeann. The latter was in 1543 created earl of Clanrickard; on his death later in the same year another Ulick, one of the contestants in 1536, assumed power and held it until the earl's son, Ricard Sassanach, the second earl of Clanrickard, came of age. The new earl extended the power of his family in Connacht by encroachments on his neighbours, the O Kellys and O Maddens – both of whom had traditionally belonged to the faction of the Lower Mac William – while he

continued the traditional alliance of his house with O
Connor Donn. Clanrickard was thus from 1543 exposed
to English influence and control, which the Lower Mac
Williams and their country, on the other hand, did not
experience until the defeat of the then ruler, Shane mac
Oliver, by the Queen's forces at the battle of Shrule in
1571. In the 1580s almost all the leading members of the
ruling house were to perish at the hands of Sir Richard
Bingham, governor of Connacht. Of the other Connacht
lords at this period, Sir Donnell O Connor of Sligo
profited by the English alliance and the contemporary
setback to O Donnell power to throw off the control of
Tirconnell and exert a suzerainty over his neighbours in
what became the county of Sligo. The O Kellys, whom
we have mentioned as increasing their territory and
power at the expense of the Berminghams and the royal
O Connors themselves in the fourteenth century, declined
in the sixteenth century, owing to a weak central chieftaincy passing between too distantly related lines. Of the
history of the O Flahertys of Iar-Connacht, the district
west of Galway, hardly anything is known before the
sixteenth century; they seem to have expanded their
territory at the expense of the Lower Mac Williams early
in that century, occupying the district between Loughs
Corrib and Mask whose immediate possessors were the
Anglo-Norman Joyces. A word might also be said
regarding two other important families of Anglo-Norman
origin; the Mac Costelloes (formerly Nangle) and the
Mac Morrises (formerly Prendergast), both in the present
County Mayo. The latter, enemies to the lower Mac
William, were hereditary allies of Clanrickard.

There is perhaps a tendency, based on the experience of
the eighteenth and nineteenth centuries, to regard Connacht
as a backwater remote from the affairs of Ireland as a
whole. As far as the medieval period is concerned, such
an impression would be wildly misleading; the province

was far from being (by Irish standards) either economically backward or politically remote and played a wholly disproportionate part in literary and religious activity. It has been remarked that the majority of surviving medieval Irish codices are of Connacht origin.

Brefny

At the period of the invasion of 1169 Tiernan O Rourke, king of Brefny, had extended his rule over the east of the kingdom of Meath, corresponding approximately to the modern county of that name. The de Lacy lords of Meath, in consequence, regarded themselves as also entitled to Brefny and by 1210 had carried their penetration so far as to occupy the central regions of County Cavan and erect castles at the ecclesiastical centre of Kilmore and even further north. Successful opposition was to come from the local family of O Reilly. In 1224 Cahal O Reilly had, by judiciously assisting the Earl Marshal against the rebel William de Lacy, managed to recover the island fortress of Lough Oughter, which Walter de Lacy had taken from him in 1220; in 1226 having slain Hugh O Rourke, he destroyed the castle of Kilmore. It was never rebuilt, and a de Lacy expedition to recover the area seven years later, after some initial successes, was repulsed with heavy loss. In 1256, however, Cahal fell with his brother, two sons and twenty others of his clan, fighting as allies of Walter de Burgo against Hugh O Connor, the king of Connacht's son, and the O Rourkes, and an O Rourke was once more made king of all Brefny. By the end of the century the O Reillys had recovered their power and under Gillisa Ruadh, chief from 1293 to 1330, consolidated their power in east Brefny, in spite of suffering two defeats (in 1305 and 1314) at the hands of the branch of the O Connors called the Clan Murtough. The latter were endeavouring at this period to establish themselves in Brefny, at first, it would seem, with some success, but after their initial friendship with the O Rourkes had been broken in 1340, a long and bitter struggle developed between the two families. After 1391 the Clan Murtough disappear from the area and the O Rourkes and O Reillys are left to divide Brefny between them. During the second half of the fourteenth century the O Reillys gradually annexed the districts around Lough Sheelin from the English of Meath; after a war in 1393 O Reilly was bribed to conclude peace, an arrangement confirmed by the Dublin government. From about the same period would appear to date the striking by the family of the coinage known as 'O Reilly's money' – in fact counterfeit English groats of base metal plated with silver – which continued through the fifteenth century. On the death of Richard O Reilly, drowned with his entourage in a boating accident on Lough Sheelin in 1418 – only O Reilly's wife, of the party, managed to swim to safety – his kinsman Owen O Reilly, whom he had previously exiled, became chief. Owen is noted as the promulgator of a code of laws – unfortunately lost – for his country. From their position the O Reillys were in close contact, alternately peaceful and hostile, with the Pale, and it is perhaps to this we may ascribe the fact that they seem to have possessed more notion of a 'state' than the average Irish lords. After 1492 the Kildare deputies interfered frequently within East Brefny, many of whose clans paid them 'buyings' (see Chapter II) for protection, and in 1526 Ferrall O Reilly was made lord by Kildare in preference to better-qualified candidates. In 1534 he was succeeded by his brother Mulmora, and he in 1566 by his son Hugh Conallach, both of whom had close relations with the English government.

In West Brefny, the O Rourke power had been consolidated by Tiernan More (died 1418) who succeeded in driving out the Clan Murtough. After his death rival lines of rulers existed for a period, but after 1458 the

O Rourkeship was reunited. At this period and later the relations of the O Rourkes, both hostile and friendly, tended to be with their neighbours to the north and west, the O Donnells, Maguires and Mac Donoghs, rather than with the O Reillys to the east.

The O Farrells of Annaly

The modern county of Longford, the medieval territory of the O Farrells, formed part of the historical province of Connacht and was grouped with Brefny as forming the *Garbhthrian* ('the rough Third') of that province. Its political history, however, is more closely linked with that of Westmeath. The area, except for its northern fringe, had been occupied by the de Lacys of Meath and passed to their de Verdon co-heirs, but in the second half of the thirteenth century a succession of able O Farrell chiefs – of whom Geoffrey (1282–1318) was the decisive figure – succeeded in destroying the settlement, which by 1300 was in ruins. During the fifteenth century the O Farrell lordship was for most of the time divided, and after the death in 1514 of the warlike bishop of Ardagh, William O Farrell, who had managed to unite the country under his rule, this division became crystallised in the formation of the two chieftaincies of O Farrell Boy (*Buidhe*) in the south and west and O Farrell Bane (*Bán*) in the north and east. The O Farrells Boy became notably loyal and their chiefs rather Anglicised in the later sixteenth century while the O Farrells Bane, on the other hand, took part in the O Neill rising at the end of the century.

9 Munster

The O Briens of Thomond

At the time of the invasion the kingdom of Thomond – or Limerick, as the invaders knew it – was ruled by Donnell Mór O Brien. On Donnell's death in 1194 the usual Irish struggle for the succession broke out between two of his sons, Murtough Fionn and Connor Ruadh. The latter was slain by Murtough's followers in 1202, but his place was taken by his full-brother Donogh Cairbreach, who succeeded in displacing Murtough in 1210, although Murtough continued to play some part in affairs until his death in 1239. Donogh Cairbreach, who had been knighted by King John, only ruled over a fragment of his father's kingdom, the region north of the Shannon corresponding to the modern county of Clare, and even in this area grants had been made to a number of Anglo-Norman lords, although settlement seems to have been confined to a few points along the Shannon itself. For this diminished kingdom Donogh paid rent to the crown. This position continued with his son Connor, who succeeded his father in 1242, but from 1248 new grants were made by King Henry III which resulted in the creation of a permanent settlement around Bunratty and Clare. It was not until 1257, however, that open war broke out between O Brien and the English, whom he defeated. This began a period of trouble in Thomond, in which the border area near Limerick, formerly peaceful, passed into a state of depopulation. In 1268 Connor O Brien was murdered, with his son and daughter, by a cousin who soon paid the price with his own life.

His successor was his son Brian Ruadh, who was soon at war with the English. In 1276 King Edward made a grant of the whole of Thomond to Thomas de Clare, a brother of the earl of Gloucester and married to the daughter and presumptive heiress of the great Geraldine baron Maurice fitz Maurice, on whose lands in County Cork he was residing. De Clare's arrival in Thomond coincided with a challenge to the power of Brian Ruadh by his nephew Turlough, and Brian Ruadh welcomed de Clare as an ally, entering into a solemn treaty with him – 'they made gossipry and mixed their blood in one vessel and bound themselves to each other upon the relics of Munster and on bells and croziers', say the annals. They seem to have been defeated by Turlough, however, and soon after de Clare – for reasons which are obscure – had Brian Ruadh treacherously seized, drawn and hanged (1277). In the following year the sons of the murdered man fell upon de Clare and defeated him at Quin, but he himself escaped and returned in the following year to erect a castle at that place. While engaged on this work he was attacked a second time, in this case by Turlough and his brother, and again defeated with the loss of many of his followers. The rise of Turlough, who was now king of Thomond, drove the sons of Brian Ruadh back into alliance with their father's murderer, and a bloody civil war raged in Thomond until Donogh mac Brian Ruadh was slain by Turlough in 1284. After this Turlough and de Clare seem to have come to an arrangement that the former should hold all of Thomond outside the Bunratty area of de Clare at a yearly rent of about £120, and this agreement was maintained down to King Turlough's death in 1306. He was succeeded by his son Donogh, who seems to have fallen out with the de Clares, perhaps through refusing to pay the agreed rent. In 1311 Richard de Clare put forward a grandson of Brian Ruadh, Dermot O Brien, as rival candidate. Donogh was assisted by Sir William Liath de Burgo, but the latter was captured in battle by de Clare and King Donogh murdered soon after by some of his own forces. Dermot ruled until 1313, after which a long struggle ensued between his cousin Donogh mac Donnell, supported by the de Clares and Murtough mac Turlough who was supported by the de Burgos and Butlers. Finally Donogh was slain in 1317 by Murtough's brother and in the following year Richard de Clare was slain by Murtough in the well-known battle of Dysert O'Dea. This was the end of the de Clares in Thomond, though the castle of Bunratty remained in English hands – with some intervals – down to the 1350s.

After Murtough's death in 1343 Brian Bán, son of the Donogh slain in 1317, was made king by the Mac Namaras, traditional supporters of his clan, but in spite of being a mighty warrior who had spent his life in very effective harrying of the English settlements of Tipperary, he was unable to maintain his position in Thomond and had to give way in 1344 to Murtough's brother Dermot. Brian Bán's position as an enemy of the Tipperary colony was inherited by his son Murrough, (died 1383), founder of the house of O Brien lords of Arra, who bore the title of Mac Uí Briain (not to be confused with the *surname* Mac Briain borne by the descendants of Brian Boru through his son Donogh, the lords of Coonagh and Aherlow in County Limerick). In 1370 Brian Sreamhach O Brien, who had succeeded his father Mahon mac Murtough as king in the preceding year, won a great victory at Monasternenagh in County Limerick against the earl of Desmond, capturing the earl and many other notables, and his vassal Mac Namara followed up the victory by taking and burning the city of Limerick. This led to a campaign by the Lord Lieutenant, Sir William de Windsor, and O Brien and Mac Namara were forced to purchase peace by a large fine, the latter agreeing among other things to allow the citizens of Limerick to take timber from his woods for the rebuilding of their city. A fresh war between O Brien and the government broke out in 1374; this time de Windsor put forward Brian's uncle Turlough Maol as a rival candidate for the kingship, and by the payment of large bribes secured the assistance of many of Brian's vassals, such as O Dea and O Connor of Corcomroe, and of his neighbour and ally, Ricard Óg de Burgo of Clanrickard. In 1375 Brian was temporarily replaced by Turlough Maol, but soon returned, and Turlough retired to pass the remainder of his life as a pensioner in the English Pale. In 1380 we hear of Brian O Brien in alliance with Ricard Óg extorting tributes from the English of Munster.

The short reign of Teig O Brien, who succeeded his father Turlough in 1459, was marked by a considerable extension of O Brien power. In 1466, the year of his death, he marched eastward across the Shannon and subjugated the lordships of the Clanwilliam Burkes – ruled by the descendants of Sir Edmond son of the Red Earl – and those of the Mac Briens along the borders of Counties Limerick and Tipperary. These territories remained under O Brien overlordship until they were surrendered to King Henry VIII in 1542. In addition, Teig managed to put the black rent paid to the O Briens by the city and county of Limerick on a fixed and permanent basis. Of his successors there is little to record – their struggle with the Kildare viceroys need not concern us here – until Murrough O Brien submitted to King Henry VIII in 1542 and was created earl of Thomond, with remainder to his nephew and tanist, Donogh. The latter, on succeeding in 1553, promptly found himself opposed by his own brothers, who saw their position threatened under the new order, and in 1553 he fell at the hands of the followers of his brother Donnell, who thereupon became O Brien. In 1558 Donnell was driven from Thomond by the earl of Sussex and replaced by the young earl Connor, Donogh's son. In 1564 Donnell returned and, in alliance with the sons of Murrough, warred with his nephew until a treaty was arranged by which he received the barony of Corcomroe in compensation for his claims on the O Brienship, which he formally renounced.

The Mac Carthys of Desmond

On the death in 1206 of Donnell Mór Mac Carthy, king of Desmond, the kingship was disputed between his brother Fineen and the late king's son Dermot. The struggle was resolved in favour of Dermot when Fineen was killed by the O Sullivans in 1209, after he had savagely harried Iveragh, but in 1212, while Dermot was a prisoner of the sheriff, Thomas Bloet, in Cork, a cousin, Cormac Óg Liathanach Mac Carthy, seized the kingship with the assistance of an army led by Donogh Cairbreach O Brien and by many of the Anglo-Normans of north Munster. Dermot was thereupon released by the sheriff, who went with him to resist Cormac, but the struggle between the rivals seems to have been, for the time being, inconclusive. It allowed, however, a massive Anglo-Norman penetration into the south-west, many castles being erected along the coast as far west as Bantry – and possibly Kenmare – while the Blackwater valley was occupied up to the borders of the present County Kerry. Dermot is described as king of Desmond at his death in 1229, but he may have been succeeded either by Cormac Liathanach (who died as a Cistercian monk in 1244) or by his own brother Cormac Fionn, who was in any case king by his death in 1247. His successor was his brother Donnell Got, who was murdered in 1252 by John fitz Thomas, apparently at the instigation of his own followers, the O Donoghues. Donnell Got had previously laid the foundation of what was to be the second Mac Carthy lordship, that of Mac Carthy Reagh, by a campaign in 1232 against the O Mahonys which resulted in his establishing himself in their territory in south-western County Cork.

Donnell Got was succeeded by his son Fineen, who warred with success against both the O Mahonys and the settlers. In 1260 he wasted Kerry and in 1261, after he had destroyed a number of frontier castles, an expedition was mounted against him by the justiciar William de Dene. On July 24, 1261, a battle took place at Callan near Kenmare in which the invaders were totally defeated, John fitz Thomas and his son Maurice falling in the battle. The tide of settlement in Desmond was permanently pushed back, and many of the border areas recovered by the Mac Carthys in consequence. Fineen went on to methodically destroy the border castles and Michaelmas of the same year saw him at Miles de Courcy's castle of Rinrone. De Courcy offered Fineen a payment to spare the place; Fineen refused it and fell in the ensuing fight. His brother and successor Cormac was slain the next year by another expedition led by Walter de Burgo, in a battle at Mangarton in which the invaders also lost heavily. Thereupon his cousin Donnell Roe (son of Cormac Fionn) who had probably been with de Burgo – as he had been with de Dene and John fitz Thomas at the defeat of Callan – became king of Desmond, a position he held until 1303. In 1280 he came to an arrangement with his cousins, Donnell Óg son of Donnell Got and Felim (grandson of Dermot who died in 1229), by which the former was conceded the country south of the Lee and the latter the districts north of Killarney. In the same year he recovered the castle of Dunloe near Killarney from the garrison which held it for John fitz Thomas's heir. In 1283 Donnell Roe secured the assistance of the Anglo-Normans of Munster against Donnell Óg, who had plotted to depose him; Carbery was devastated and its rule given to a nephew of Donnell Óg, who, however, soon returned. In 1285 Donnell Roe captured Donnell Óg, but released him on obtaining his submission.

Donnell Roe's successor was his brother Donogh, who was deposed by his subjects in 1310 in favour of his grandnephew Dermot. Dermot took advantage of the confusion produced by the Bruce invasion in 1316 to raid Kerry; in the following year he successfully resisted a bid to displace him by his uncle Dermot Roe. He was murdered at Tralee in 1325 by some of the gentry of Kerry and was succeeded by his brother Cormac, who had a long and successful reign. In 1352 he co-operated with the justiciar Sir Thomas de Rokeby in a campaign against his kinsman Dermot mac Dermot Mac Carthy, an ally of the earl of Desmond and whose territories lay on Cormac's eastern frontier. Dermot was defeated and in February, 1352, Cormac received a grant from the crown of extensive lands on his eastern and northern borders which were to become the foundations of the lordships of Muskerry and Coshmang, belonging respectively to the descendants of Cormac's second and third sons, Dermot and Owen. Cormac died in 1359; his son and successor Donnell (died 1392) continued his father's policy of seeking favours from the adminstration; in 1365, as 'captain of the Irish of Desmond' he obtained from the Lord Lieutenant, the duke of Clarence, a confirmatory grant of his lands. After Donnell's death the succession of the Mac Carthys Mór – as they were styled – passed from father to son for four generations until the death of Donnell in 1508, when a succession war broke out between his brother Cormac and son Teig until the latter's death in 1514. Donnell Mac Carthy Mór was created earl of Clancare in 1565; on his death in 1596 the title of Mac Carthy Mór was claimed both by his natural son Donnell – the best entitled by Irish law – and by

Fineen Mac Carthy of the house of Mac Carthy Reagh, who had married the earl's legitimate daughter (and heiress by English law).

Throughout the fifteenth and sixteenth centuries the Mac Carthys Mór were consistent enemies of the earls of Desmond, who claimed – with more or less success – a tribute out of Desmond. (It is interesting to note that at this period the name 'Desmond' was applied to just that part of south Munster in which the earls of Desmond had least control.) The same applied to the other great Mac Carthy houses, with the exception, perhaps, of the Mac Donogh Mac Carthys, lords of Duhallow, who descended from the Dermot mac Dermot of 1352 mentioned above. The Mac Carthys Reagh of Carbery, descendants of Donnell Got, were enemies both of Mac Carthy Mór and of the earls of Desmond, who likewise claimed a tribute from their territory. A long succession struggle in the late fifteenth century had not weakened their power, and a succession of able chiefs preserved their lordship strong and intact down to the end of the sixteenth century. The origin of the lords of Muskerry has been already referred to. They were a grasping and politically able house who in the fifteenth and sixteenth centuries became one of the most influential in Munster and who consistently sought alliance with the English crown. The nucleus of Muskerry was the land around Macroom which had been granted by King Edward III in 1353 (see above); its lords had expanded eastwards during the fifteenth century, at the expense of the Anglo-Norman Barrets and of the Lombards of Cork, from whom they took Blarney some time in the second half of the century, and southwards at the expense of the Gaelic O Mahonys. The lords of Muskerry during this period were Cormac mac Teig, murdered by his own brother Owen in 1495, and his son Cormac Óg (died 1536), who with the assistance of Sir Thomas of Desmond slew Owen in

1498 and in 1524, in alliance with Mac Carthy Reagh and the same Sir Thomas, the earl's uncle, defeated the earl of Desmond at the battle of Mourne Abbey. These lords of Muskerry figure prominently in the Irish politics of the time, and their successors seem to have been equally able.

The earls of Desmond and the Anglo-Norman lords of Munster

The founder of the line of the Desmond Geraldines was Thomas fitz Maurice, one of the sons of the original invader Maurice fitz Gerald. Thomas's son – by a Gaelic wife – was John fitz Thomas, who inherited his father's lands, mainly in western Limerick, and immensely increased his possessions by marrying one of the daughters of Thomas fitz Anthony, a Leinster baron to whom Decies and Desmond with the hereditary sergeantship of Counties Cork and Waterford had been granted by King John. The lion's share of fitz Anthony's possessions in Munster passed to John fitz Thomas and his wife, while he also acquired Trughanacmy in Kerry and other lands. His death along with his eldest son at the battle of Callan in 1261 (see above) and the long minority of his grandson and heir led to the loss of the more south-westerly lands to the Irish. The grandson, Thomas fitz Maurice, was the father of the famous Maurice fitz Thomas, first earl of Desmond. Although most of his life was spent in effectively destroy-ing the royal authority in Munster, he was created earl of Desmond in 1329 and had in the same year a grant of the county of Kerry as a liberty for himself and his heirs. Like his successors, he extended his lands by buying up those of absentees, though he was unsuccessful in his attempt to recover from the Mac Carthys the lands in the extreme south-west of County Cork. He died in 1355. His son and successor Maurice, who married an English wife, was probably more anglicised, but he was drowned three years later and – the next brother being an idiot – the succession passed to the first earl's third son, Gerald. Earl Gerald, although he served as Justiciar of Ireland from 1367 to 1369, was deeply immersed in Gaelic culture. He is credited with being the originator of Gaelic love poetry, and his children – to judge from the story later related of his daughter Katherine Desmond (see Chapter IV), which depicts her as totally unaccustomed to English dress, as well as by the fact that his son James (afterwards earl) was fostered by O Brien of Thomond – were brought up as Gaelic Irish. His eldest son John, having succeeded his father in 1398, was drowned within the year on his way home from a campaign against his uncle the earl of Ormond. John's son Thomas was expelled in 1411 by his uncle James and died an exile in France in 1420. James, who thus became earl, consolidated his territories and established the power of the earldom on the basis of the Gaelic exaction of 'coyne', the cessing of troops and followers on the country, which he placed on a regular footing. He divided the family territories, however, by granting Decies to his younger son Garret, who was to found the house of the lords of the Decies, the Fitz Geralds of Dromana. Earl James died in 1462; his son and successor Thomas became Lord Deputy in 1463. As a Yorkist Deputy he was able to use his position to war against his enemies the Lancastrian Butlers, with whom his father had previously conducted a long war in the 1440s. In 1467, after his removal from office, he was suddenly seized and executed by the new Deputy, Tiptoft. His brother Garret in revenge conducted a great campaign in Meath, wasting and plundering the country in alliance with the Irish of Leinster, but soon returned to Munster to attempt to oust his nephew, Thomas' son James, on the grounds that the dispensation granted for his parents' marriage had been defective. He failed, however, either to establish this in law or to oust his nephew by force, and the latter was established as earl in 1470 with the help of the Mac Carthys and O Briens. In 1487 he was murdered, allegedly at the instigation of his own brother John, and another brother, Maurice, became earl. Although a cripple, the new earl was a strong and effective ruler, as was his son and successor James, who, however, had to contend with the hostility of his own uncles, Sir Thomas and Sir John, as well as that of his cousin John fitz Garret of the Decies, who resisted the earl's efforts to assert his suzerainty over that area. Sir Thomas was with the Mac Carthys when they defeated the earl in the decisive battle of Mourne Abbey in 1524. He himself became earl on his nephew's death in 1529 and promptly entered into a treaty with his cousins of the Decies in which he conceded most of their claims, renouncing authority over their country and agreeing to refer further disputes to arbitration. The lords of the Decies were to survive into the seventeenth century. On his death in 1534 his brother Sir John seized the earldom, in spite of the existence of a grandson of his predecessor, and was succeeded in 1536 by his son James. Thomas's grandson, another James, who had been brought up in England, came over to Ireland on his grandfather's death and was supported by the latter's old friend, Cormac Óg Mac Carthy of Muskerry, whose daughter he married; he achieved no success, however, and was slain in 1540 by the *de facto* earl's brother, Maurice fitz John. On Earl James's death in 1558 his eldest son, Sir Thomas of Conna, whose mother had been divorced by the earl, was set aside on this pretext in favour of his younger half-brother Gerald, the last recognised earl, who fell as a hunted fugitive in 1583.

The power of the earls of Desmond was centred in County Limerick and in central Kerry, but other areas which they ruled directly were scattered through County Cork and their influence, of course, extended over a much wider area. In northern Kerry their relationship with their kinsmen, the Fitz Maurices (Mac Muiris), was an ambiguous one, the Fitz Maurices – although recognised as hereditary marshals to the earl – resisting Desmond's claims to authority over their territory to the extent of denying that it formed part of the liberty of Kerry. The text of two interesting treaties regulating their relations, from 1421 and 1541, has been preserved.[8] Of the other Anglo-Norman lords of south Munster the most important were the Barrys, whose heads were styled Barry Mór (an Barrach Mór) in Irish and Viscount Buttevant in English (the alleged viscountcy, like that assumed by the Roches of Fermoy, had no real foundation). After 1557 the headship passed, by an arrangement which excluded the nearer male heirs, to James fitz Richard Barry Roe, the chief of another branch whose territory of Ibawn lay among the Gaelic Irish in the extreme south-west and paid tribute to Mac Carthy Reagh. The third ruling branch of the Barrys was that of Barry Óg, lords of Kinelea; the 'simplicity' and weakness of Sir Thomas Barry Óg (died 1590) reduced him to 'a poor beggarly captain of a country' (as he is styled in 1579) and brought about the ruin of his family. Next in importance to the Barrys were the Roches and Condons, two families who shared the territory of Fermoy and whose enmity to each other went back to the thirteenth century. The Courcys of Kinsale, once great, had been reduced by the encroachments of Mac Carthy Reagh to a very small territory. The Barrets, whose scattered lands lay along the frontiers of Muskerry, paid tribute to Mac Carthy Mór. Of more importance than some of these lords were the various Geraldine chiefs under the earls of Desmond; the knights of Kerry, the knights of Glin in northern Limerick, and the White Knights on the borders of Limerick and Cork. These curious titles go back to the beginning of the fifteenth century. Another Geraldine house of importance was that of the hereditary seneschals of Imokilly in County Cork, whose home was Castle-martyr.

The Butler territories

The territories ruled by the Butler earls of Ormond in the later middle ages cut across any provincial classification, for – as the statutes issued by the White Earl of Ormond in 1433 declared – the counties of Tipperary and Kilkenny were treated as 'one country under one government and one lord'. County Tipperary had been erected into a liberty for the first earl of Ormond in 1328; the power exercised by his successors in the county of Kilkenny, after their acquisition of Kilkenny itself from its absentee owners in 1392 (they already, of course, held extensive lands in the county), was solely due to its remoteness from Dublin and the consequent inability of the adminstration to exercise any degree of control there. In their adminstration, the Butler territories – a fact often slurred over – were quite Gaelicised, the earls employing – from at least 1432 – Gaelic brehons to adminster justice.

The foundation of the Butler lordship had been the various territories granted or confirmed by King John to Theobald Walter, the founder of the family in Ireland. These included the whole of the northern half of County Tipperary, including Ely O Carroll. This entire area had been parcelled out into fiefs – the thoroughness of the settlement is shown, for instance, by the survey of Ely O Carroll made in 1305 – and many manorial villages and communities had come into existence. In the early fourteenth century the situation in this area was to alter drastically. Teig O Carroll, prince of Ely, was able to 'slay, exile and eject from his lands of Ely O Carroll those of the nations of Barry, of Milbourne, of Brett, and the other English of the country, and to hold and occupy their lands and castles and be a heavy tyrant to the lieges of the neighbourhood' and his death in battle at the hands of

Ormond's seneschal in 1346 did not alter the situation; the O Carrolls retained Ely down to the time of James I. In 1515 they were receiving an annual black rent from the counties of Kilkenny and Tipperary. The collapse of the colony in Ormond proper was more gradual; successive fourteenth-century treaties between the earls and the O Kennedys recognise the latter's independence more and more clearly, but throughout the fifteenth century the area continued to pay a heavy tribute in cattle to the earls while the O Kennedys recognised that they held the castle of Nenagh as the earl's constables. After 1540 the earls gradually reasserted their authority in the area, but failed to do so in the neighbouring Ely O Carroll, which the O Carrolls after a long struggle finally (in 1606) succeeded in having excluded from the liberty of Tipperary and added to King's County.

The history of the Butlers as an independent power really begins with James, third earl of Ormond, who acquired Kilkenny in 1392 and from whose time, also, date the perennial wars which raged between the earls of Ormond and Desmond. After his death in 1404 the new earl – James, known as the 'White Earl' – was involved in a war with his cousin Katherine of Desmond, who had been wife (after the Irish fashion) to her uncle the earl of Ormond and who was by later tradition reputed to have poisoned the latter's English countess, the new earl's mother (see Chapter IV). In this war, Tipperary was again ravaged, while the Burkes of Clanwilliam – with whom Ormond had entered into a treaty in 1401 – attacked County Kilkenny in alliance with O Carroll, but were defeated. The new earl, however, soon established his authority. In 1433 he published at Fethard a series of statutes for Counties Kilkenny and Tipperary and appointed his half-brother James Gallda Butler (Katherine's son) as keeper of the peace of County Tipperary. In 1445 there was a great war between Ormond and Desmond in which each ravaged the other's territories. The White Earl died in 1452 and his three sons – who in turn succeeded as earl – were absentees, deeply involved (on the Lancastrian side) in English politics, who left the management of their Irish territories in the hands of their kinsfolk. The principal of these were Edmond mac Richard Butler of Paulstown (died 1462), whose grandson eventually succeeded to the earldom, the Butlers of Cahir, descendants of James Gallda, and the barons of Dunboyne, whose head bore the Irish title of Mac Piarais (from an ancestor, Piers Butler) and who held the seneschalsy of the liberty of Tipperary almost as a hereditary office. Between the house of Cahir and the other two lines there subsisted an inveterate hostility. All three lines were more or less Gaelicised, having intermarried with the Gaelic Irish and being patrons of Irish scribes and poets. The well-known Irish manuscript known as the Book of Mac Richard, now in the Bodleian Library, was written for Edmond mac Richard Butler at his castle of Pottlerath in County Kilkenny and after the defeat of the Butlers by the earl of Desmond at Pilltown in 1462 passed into the hands of the latter.

After the death in 1486 of James Butler, who had succeeded to the position of his father Edmond mac Richard, a struggle for the position as representative of the absentee seventh earl developed between his son Piers Ruadh and Sir James Dubh Butler, the natural son (by an O Brien) of the sixth earl. The latter was in by far the stronger position, but in 1497 he was attacked and killed by his rival. On the death of the seventh earl in 1515 the latter became earl of Ormond, as he was already undisputed head of the Irish Butlers, although from 1528 to 1537 he was to resign the Ormond title – wanted by King Henry VIII for Anne Boleyn's father – for that of earl of Ossory.

The Mac Gillapatricks had been kings of Ossory

before the invasion. During the thirteenth century they had remained entrenched in the mountains of Slieve Bloom, and during the fourteenth century they succeeded in recovering the country as far as the present border of County Kilkenny. This was known as Upper Ossory. Although a powerful family possessed of extensive territories, their history is, strangely, almost completely unknown. They were enemies of the people of County Kilkenny and of the Butlers and for this reason managed in the sixteenth century to have their territory annexed to the newly created Queen's County. Brian Mac Gilla-patrick – or, as the surname was to become, Fitz Patrick, was created by King Henry VIII baron of Upper Ossory, a title retained by his descendants.

10   Leinster and Meath

The Mac Murroughs, kings of Leinster

It is perhaps ironical that Dermot Mac Murrough's kingship of Leinster should have been the last of the old provincial kingships to remain as a title in use, as it did down to the end of the sixteenth century. After Dermot's death, his nephew Murtough had been recognised by Richard Strongbow as king of Uí Cinnsealaigh, presumably of the district in north Wexford known in later times as Kinsellagh, where Anglo-Norman penetration seems to have been slight, except along the coast, even in the heyday of the Leinster colony in the early thirteenth century. Murtough died in 1192, and thereafter there is a gap in our information regarding the Mac Murroughs until the 1270s, when another Murtough, styled king of Leinster, and his brother Art appear as disturbers of the peace in what is now County Wicklow. Although figuring as rebels, they seem to have been protégés of the earl of Norfolk, as lord of the liberty of Carlow, and when they were killed – in circumstances savouring of treachery – at Arklow in 1282, he was to protest to the King at the act. The Mac Murrough kings at this period enjoyed in fact a recognised position in the liberty of Carlow as heads of the Irishry. After 1300 relations seem to have grown worse, and through most of the fourteenth century our notices of the Mac Murroughs are a record of successive kings of Leinster – whose genealogy is usually unknown – being killed by the Englishry or captured and executed, or occasionally serving as allies of the adminstration against their own kin. In the district of Kinsellagh a number of collateral lines of the house came into existence, those represented later by the houses of Kinsellagh, Mac Vadock and Mac David Mór (a title, not a surname; the family, known as the Clann Réamuinn from a Raymond Mac Murrough who was tenant to the crown in Courtown between 1309 and 1334, assumed in the early seventeenth century the surname of Redmond).

With the accession, some time in the 1370s, of the famous Art Mór Mac Murrough, the position changed sharply. By his death in 1416, Art had created a solid and coherent kingdom covering northern Wexford and most of County Carlow, in spite of the attempts of the administration, and of King Richard II on his visit to Ireland, to restrain or remove him. His occupation of the Barrow valley south of Carlow was of especial political significance, as it effectively cut the communications between Dublin and the south-west of the country. Although Art's son and successor Donogh, having been captured by the Lord Lieutenant Talbot, was a prisoner of the English from 1419 to 1427, his brother Gerald took his place and continued to levy the black rents which the Mac Murroughs received both from the central Exchequer in Dublin and from the county of Wexford. Donogh was released in 1427 and, Gerald having died in 1430, continued to reign until 1450 at least. In 1442, his son Murtough having been slain by the English of County Wexford – probably while raiding them – he levied an *eric* of 800 marks from that county in consequence. Donogh's successor was his nephew Donnell Reagh (son of Gerald), who died from the effects of a broken leg in 1475 or 1476. His successor seems to have been Murrough Ballach, grandson of Donough, who died as king of Leinster in 1511 and was succeeded in turn by three sons of Donnell Reagh, Art Buidhe (Boy), who died in 1517, Gerald (died 1522) and Maurice. In 1525 Maurice entered into an agreement with the earl of Ormond by which he agreed to surrender to the earl the castle and manor of Arklow, which must have been taken by the Mac Murroughs from the Butlers some time in the fifteenth century. In return the earl agreed that Maurice should receive half its rents and profits during his life. On Maurice's death in 1531 Cahir 'mac Inycross', probably a natural son of Murrough Ballach and a follower of the earl of Kildare, was made Mac Murrough by the latter, in opposition to a rival claimant. In 1536 he entered into indentures with the Lord Deputy, Lord Leonard Grey, by which he surrendered Ferns and some other places to the Crown. Another Cahir, Cahir mac Art, who became Mac Murrough on the death of Murtough mac Art Boy in 1547, was in 1554 created baron of Ballyanne for life, while his tanist, Murrough (son of the Maurice who had died in 1531) was, on succeeding, to be similarly created baron of Coolnaleen. Cahir died in the same year, and Murrough accordingly succeeded, but in 1557 was seized and executed by the Lord Deputy earl of Sussex. He was the last Mac Murrough recognised by the crown. Thereafter the family were brought under the authority of the crown, especially by the ruthless Thomas Masterson, constable of Ferns, who put many of them to death. Murrough's son Crehon (Criomhthann) is said to have been 'in election as king of Leinster'; he was executed at Dublin in 1582 on charges of having assisted the rebel Lord Baltinglass. The title of king was last assumed, during the O Neill rebellion, by Donnell Spáineach (so called because he had spent part of his youth as a protégé of Thomas Stukely in Spain) who nevertheless made peace with the government in 1603 and remained the most important man of his name until his death in 1631.

Before the invasion the O Byrnes had been lords of Uí
Faoláin (Offelan), in the north-east of County Kildare,
and the O Tooles of Uí Muireadhaigh (Omurthy) in the
south of that county and extending eastwards to the
mountains. The O Tooles remained settled in Imaal as
feudal tenants to the Anglo-Norman lords throughout
the thirteenth century, while others were recognised as
landholders under the archbishop of Dublin; there is
constant reference, however, to members of the family
as felons and outlaws in the later thirteenth century and
after 1300 they were open enemies of the crown and the
settlers. Having reoccupied all Imaal they spread eastwards
of the Wicklow mountains to occupy the districts of
Fartir and Fercullen (Powerscourt). In 1542 Turlough
O Toole of Powerscourt and his brother Art Óg of
Castlekevin (in Fartir) submitted to the King and received
regrants of their lands. The early movements of the
O Byrnes are uncertain; one branch established themselves in County Carlow, where they remained as important followers of the Mac Murroughs down to the
end. The chiefs of the name, with many of their followers,
turn up in 1307 as tenants in the barony of Wicklow; the
context shows that they were refusing to pay their rent
to its lords. From here they gradually moved northwards,
occupying the area which for some time in the fourteenth
century had looked like becoming a marcher lordship
under the Anglo-Norman clan of Lawless and eventually
establishing their northern frontier at Delgany, while
their territory stretched to include Shillelagh on the south.
The last recognised chief of the O Byrnes was Teig Óg,
who died in 1578; on his death the government refused
to recognise his successor and installed Sir Henry Harring-
ton as seneschal of the country, with the powers formerly
held by the chief. The branch of the O Byrnes known
as the *Gabhail Raghnaill* (Gowlranell) only rose to im-

portance in the sixteenth century, under their chiefs
Hugh mac Shane and Feagh mac Hugh.

Leix and Offaly

The O Mores of Leix and the O Connors of Offaly figure
prominently in the history of the settlement as enemies
of the Pale and of County Kildare. They were the first
two Irish powers to be destroyed by the English government during the sixteenth century reconquest. Much of
the history of the O Mores is obscure. After a period during
which they had held western Leix as the recognised
tenants of its Mortimer lords, the family reconquered
the whole area in the middle of the fourteenth century,
extending their conquests to include Slievemargy, which
had been no part of their pre-invasion territory. The
O Connors of Offaly figure much more prominently
in the sources, both English and Irish. The murder of
Murtough O Connor and his brother Calvagh by Sir
Piers de Bermingham in his castle at Carrickeoris in 1305
was long remembered as an act of hideous treachery. This
Murtough's son, Murtough Óg, succeeded a cousin
Cahir some time after 1366 and was himself succeeded in
1382 by his son Murrough, an able ruler who warred
against the English of Meath. The black rent which the
O Connors were to receive from that county probably
dated from his time. In 1421 he was succeeded by his son
Calvagh, who ruled until 1458. During his time one of
the principal seats of the O Connors was the castle of
Rathangan, which they had taken from the earls of
Kildare; it was probably recovered by the latter as a
consequence of the defeat and capture of Calvagh's
son and successor Conn by Earl Thomas of Kildare in
1459. In the following year, however, having been
released, he inflicted a great defeat on the men of Meath.
In 1471 his half-brother Teig revolted and attacked him
with the assistance of an English force, but died in the

same year. In 1511 Conn's son and successor Cahir was slain by the sons of Teig, two of whom, Brian (died 1517) and Calvagh ruled in succession as protégés of the earl of Kildare. By 1525 Calvagh had been replaced by Cahir's son, the famous Brian, the last lord of Offaly before the plantation. Neighbours and tributaries of the O Connors to the south were the O Dempseys of Clanmaliere and the O Dunnes of Iregan (see Chapter II). Both escaped the ruin of the O Connors in the mid-sixteenth century to survive into the seventeenth century.

In or around 1367 the rebel Berminghams of Carbury established an independent marcher lordship on the north-eastern frontier of the O Connors, which during the fifteenth century was to figure alternately as an ally of the O Connors in plundering Meath and as an ally (no doubt hired) of the Meathmen against the O Connors. In 1368 they had forced the release of James de Bermingham, a prisoner in irons in the castle of Trim on account of the robberies which they had committed in Meath the previous year, by capturing the chancellor of Ireland, the sheriff of Meath and others and holding them until the exchange was arranged. Carbury was the first independent Gaelicised lordship to be suppressed by the government in the reconquest of the sixteenth century. Sir William Bermingham, the then chief by tanistry – not by primogeniture succession – had been created a baron by King Henry VIII; on his death in 1548, leaving only an infant son (who died soon after) the adminstration seized the opportunity to extinguish the lordship.

The Westmeath lordships

At the date of the invasion the O Melaghlins, kings of Meath, had already lost the eastern part of the province to Tiernan O Rourke and were in possession only of the western part, which besides the present Westmeath included also the central and western part of County

Offaly. The expansion of the colony after 1200 reduced them to wanderers in the boggy, wooded country of Delvin Mac Coghlan. Cormac mac Art O Melaghlin, who died in 1239, was a noted warrior against the settlers, but although tanist, was never king. His son Art, nominal king of Meath, continued his father's war against the English, and was reputed to have destroyed twenty-seven castles in the course of his career. On his death in 1283 he was succeeded by his son Carbry, also a successful enemy of the settlers, who in 1289 decisively defeated an expedition – including Manus O Connor, king of Connacht – led against him by the Justiciar John de Sandford. Among those who fell was Richard Tuite, the head of the family which claimed to be lords of all the area occupied at this time by the O Melaghlins and their followers. The head of their barony in this area was the castle of Ballyloughloe. Carbry was murdered in 1290, not without provocation, by his own vassals the Mac Coghlans. The fact that the earl of Ulster revenged his death shows that, like most Irish chiefs of the period, he had his allies as well as his enemies among the settlers. During the fourteenth century the Tuites were expelled from the area, which was recovered by the Irish, but the beneficiaries were the immediate old possessors of the various districts; the Magawleys of Calry, who took possession of Ballyloughloe itself, situated in their little territory of Calry, the O Breens of Brawny and the Mac Coghlans of Delvin. The Magawleys and Mac Coghlans remained vassals of the O Melaghlins down to the middle of the sixteenth century, but the lands directly in the hands of the latter were too small in extent to be the foundation of an effective power. Their decline in the sixteenth century was helped by the violent fratricidal wars which raged among them at this period.

The O Molloys of Fercall occupied an extensive territory of woodland and bog in which Norman settlement had never penetrated beyond the south-west fringe near Birr. The Mageoghagans of Kineleagh (*Cinéal Fhiacha*) play a part in affairs much greater than the small size of their territory (the modern barony of Moycashell in County Westmeath) would suggest. The area had been densely occupied by settlers in the thirteenth century, and the Mageoghagans would appear to have been very much a new family who built up a lordship through expelling the settlers. The Gaelicised Norman lordships of West-meath, which came into existence towards the close of the fourteenth century, were those of the Daltons, Dillons, Tyrrells and Delamares (who were in Irish called Mac Oireabaird). Of these the Daltons would appear to have been the first to reject the authority of the Dublin govern-ment, towards the close of the fourteenth century, and the Delamares the last, after the middle of the fifteenth. The Dillons, from 1398 onwards, held the royal castle of Athlone as hereditary constables, but lost it for considerable periods to their neighbours on the west, the O Kellys. The Tyrrell captaincy would appear to have been extinguished by the crown after the death of Sir Thomas Tyrrell *circa* 1562; in 1570, after the death of the chief of the Daltons, an English seneschal was appointed to rule their country with the perquisites and authority of the former chief, and the same course was followed with the Dillons in 1578. The elective Delamare chieftaincy continued until after 1590.

Bibliography

As has been observed, there are no good general works on the history or institutions of late medieval Gaelic Ireland and very few articles worthy of recommendation on either local history or specific aspects of society, other than literature. To give a critical discussion of the source material, which is largely unpublished, would be impossible in the space available here. Some outdated works, such as W. F. T. Butler, *Gleanings from Irish History*, London, 1925, contain valuable information but are dangerously misleading.

Political and legal institutions

There are, as has been said, no general works and very few monographs which can be recommended. An exception is G. Mac Niocaill, 'A propos du vocabulaire social Irlandais du Bas Moyen Age', *Études Celtiques*, xii (1970–71), pp. 512–46, dealing with some titles and terms of rank found in Gaelic sources. On the inauguration of chiefs see G. A. Hayes-McCoy, 'The making of an O'Neill: a view of the ceremony at Tullaghoge, County Tyrone', *Ulster Journal of Archaeology*, 3rd ser., xxxiii (1970), pp. 89–94, while H. F. Hore, 'Inauguration of Irish Chiefs', in *ibid.*, 1st ser., v (1857), pp. 216–35, may still also be consulted. On legal questions there is little literature. G. Mac Niocaill, 'Notes on Litigation in late Irish Law', *Irish Jurist*, new ser., ii (1967), pp. 299–307, deals comprehensively with one aspect. On 'Irish gavelkind' and a few other legal points, see my introduction to 'Some Documents on Irish Law and Custom in the Sixteenth Century', *Analecta Hibernica*, xxvi (1970), pp. 103–29. M. Graham, 'Rural Society in Connacht, 1600–1640', in *Irish Geographical Studies in honour of E. Estyn Evans* ed. Nicholas Stephens and Robin E. Glascock, Q.U.B. 1970, pp. 192–208, is useful on some points concerning landownership, but the writer unfortunately lacks understanding of the legal and social background. For Irish law and the exactions of lords, the presentments of 1537 and after, printed by H. J. Hore and the Rev. J. Graves as 'The Social State of the Southern and Eastern Counties of Ireland in the Sixteenth Century' (*Annuary of the Kilkenny and South-East of Ireland Archaeological Society*, 1858, *Annuary of the Royal Historical and Archaeological Association of Ireland*, 1868–69) are invaluable; unfortunately the work is extremely scarce. The notes are not to be relied upon. Translations of many important sixteenth-century documents are to be found in the *Calendar of Carew MSS*, ed. J. S. Brewer and W. Bullen, London, 1867 especially Vol. I and the supplementary volume (*Book of Howth*, etc.), and originals in the *State Papers of Henry VIII*, iii (1834). Others can be found printed in the *Calendar of Ormond Deeds*, i–vi, ed. E. Curtis, Dublin 1932–43 (where abstracts only are given, these are frequently incorrect or omit the most important parts of the originals) and in *Irish Monastic and Episcopal Deeds*, ed. N. B. White, Dublin 1936, while occasional documents are to be found printed elsewhere, e.g. in *The Miscellany of the Irish Archaeological Society*, i (1846). The Kerrycurrihy document referred to in Chapter IV is to be found in R. Caulfield, *The Council Book of the Corporation of Kinsale*, Guildford 1879, pp. 423–5.

Social and descriptive

Sixteenth-century English accounts of Irish manners and customs are to be found best collected, so far as their essential parts are concerned, in D. B. Quinn, *The Elizabethans and the Irish*, New York 1966, pp. 34–105. For two earlier accounts (including that of Perelhos in 1397) see J. P. Mahaffy, 'Two early tours in Ireland', *Hermathena*, xviii (1914), pp. 1–16, and for some slightly later ones, C. Litton Falkiner, *Illustrations of Irish History*, London 1904. For native Irish domestic architecture, see C. Ó Danachair, 'Representations of Houses on some Irish Maps of *circa* 1600', in *Studies in Folk Life: Essays in honour of Iorwerth C. Peate*, ed. G. Jenkins, London 1969, pp. 91–103; for castles, H. G. Leask, *Irish Castles and Castellated Houses*, 2nd ed. Dundalk 1944; on costume, H. F. McClintock, *Old Irish and Highland Dress*, 2nd ed. Dundalk 1950 (he seems, however, to have been unaware of Perelhos' account mentioned above); on Irish woods, E. McCracken, 'The Woodlands of Ireland *circa* 1600', in *Irish Historical Studies*, xi (1958–59), pp. 271–96 (not exhaustive). On military matters, G. A. Hayes-McCoy, *Scots Mercenary Forces in Ireland, 1565–1603*, Dublin 1937 (marred only by the writer's belief in the division of the population into rigidly defined 'free' and 'unfree' classes); *idem*, 'The Galloglach Axe', *Galway Archaeological Soc. Journal*, xvii (1936–37), pp. 101–21; *idem*, 'The Early History of Guns in Ireland', *ibid.*, xviii (1938–39), pp. 43–65. On the galloglass, see in particular A. McKerral, 'West Highland Mercenaries in Ireland', *Scottish Historical Review*, xxx (1951), pp. 1–14. There are no general works on any aspect of economic life. Some interesting information on Irish agriculture at a slightly later period (the late seventeenth century) can be found in Sir Henry Piers' 'A Chorographical Description of the County of Westmeath' (1682), in Vallancey, *Collectanea de Rebus Hibernicis*, i, 1770. See also E. MacLysaght, *Irish Life in the Seventeenth Century*, Cork 1939 repr. 1969, pp. 166–82, and E. E. Evans, *Irish Folk Ways*, London 1957.

On the church, a good general survey is in C. Mooney, O.F.M., 'The Church in Gaelic Ireland, 13th to 15th Centuries', (*A History of Irish Catholicism*, ii, 5), 1969. For the Gaelic Ulster dioceses at the close of the period see the two invaluable descriptions by Bishop George Montgomery, one printed in *Ordnance Survey of the County of Londonderry*, i (*Parish of Templemore*), 1837, pp. 49–52, the other (ed. A. F. O'D. Alexander) in 'The O'Kane Papers', *Analecta Hibernica*, xii, pp. 81–111 (the translation is sometimes poor). A. O. Gwynn, *The Medieval Province of Armagh, 1470–1545*, Dundalk 1946 and W. Reeves, *Acts of Archbishop Colton in his Metropolitan Visitation of the Diocese of Derry*, Dublin 1850, are very useful. On the origin of the parish system in Gaelic Ireland see my article, 'Rectory, Vicarage and Parish in the Western Irish Dioceses', *Journal of the Royal Society of Antiquaries of Ireland*, ci (1971). The great printed source is of course the *Calendar of Papal Registers: Letters*; London 1893–1960 see also the calendars which have been printed of some (not all) of the Armagh archiepiscopal registers: H. J. Lawlor, 'A Calendar of the Register of Archbishop Sweteman', *Proceedings of the Royal Irish Academy*, xxix C (1911), 213–310; *idem*, 'A Calendar of the Register of Archbishop Fleming', *ibid.*, xxx C (1912), pp. 94–190; D. A. Chart, *The Register of John Swayne*, Belfast 1935. There are many works on the religious orders. See especially the writings of Fr Colmcille Conway, including *The Story of Mellifont*, Dublin 1958, and those of B. W. O'Dwyer, including *The Conspiracy of Mellifont*, Dublin Historical Association's Medieval Irish History series, 2, 1970. For the observant movement among the Irish friars see F. X. Martin, 'The Irish Augustinian Reform Movement in the fifteenth Century', in *Medieval Studies presented to Aubrey Gwynn*, ed. J. A. Watt, J. B. Morrall, F. X. Martin, Dublin 1961, pp. 230–64. On papal provisions see U. G. Flanagan, 'Papal Letters of the Fifteenth Century as a Source for Irish History', *Irish Catholic Historical Committee Proc.*, 1958, pp. 11–5; *idem*, 'Papal Provisions in Ireland, 1305–78', *Historical Studies*, iii (1961), pp. 92–103; R. D. Edwards, 'The Kings of England and Papal Provisions in Fifteenth-Century Ireland', *Medieval Studies presented to Aubrey Gwynn*, pp. 265–80. None of the numerous writings on the system of coarbs and erenaghs can be recommended, and there is nothing in print on some of the other important topics, such as tithes or the secular use of churches.

On literature one can recommend as an introduction *Seven Centuries of Irish Learning*, ed. B. Ó Cuiv, Cork 1961 repr. 1970. P. Walsh, *Irish Men of Learning*, Dublin 1947, is useful as a collection of essays on some members of the learned classes.

On the historical side, one must refer the reader to the original sources, especially the Irish Annals, the principal being the *Annals of the Kingdom of Ireland by the Four Masters*, ed. and trans. John O'Donovan, Dublin 1848–51; *The Annals of Loch Cé*, ed. and trans. W. M. Hennessy, London 1871; *The Annals of Ulster*, ed. and trans. W. M. Hennessy and B. MacCarthy, Dublin 1887–1901; *The Annals of Connacht*, ed. and trans. A. M. Freeman, Dublin 1944; *Miscellaneous Irish Annals*, ed. and trans. S. Ó hInnse, Dublin 1947; and *The Annals of Innisfallen*, ed. and trans. S. MacAirt, Dublin 1951. The translations are not always to be relied upon, those of *Loch Cé* and *Ulster* being especially bad. Preserved only in seventeenth-century English translation are *The Annals of Clonmacnoise*, ed. D. Murphy, Dublin 1896, and 'Annals of Ireland, from the year 1443 to 1468, translated from the Irish by Dudley Firbisse', ed. J. O'Donovan, in *The Miscellany of the Irish Archaeological Society*, i (1846), pp. 198–302. There are few studies on local history. Goddard H. Orpen, 'The Normans in Tirowen and Tirconnell', in *J.R.S.A.I.*, xlv (1915), pp. 275–88, is useful for those areas during the thirteenth century. A fourteenth-century Irish history of the wars in Thomond, *Caithréim Thoirdhealbhaigh*, *The Triumphs of Turlough*, by John Magrath, ed. and trans. S. H. O'Grady, London 1929, 2 vols. (Irish Texts Society 1924–25), is not always historically accurate but gives a valuable picture of society. The articles collected in P. Walsh, *Irish Chiefs and Leaders*, Dublin 1960, may be recommended (with some reservations). Some other good articles may also be found scattered through the local archaeological journals; some, especially those of more recent date, are of moderately good quality, many very poor.

Glossary

allodial: In France and other European countries the term 'allod' (*allodium*, *alleu*) denoted land which was held in absolute proprietorship and not feudally, of a superior.

In England, on the other hand, all land was supposed to be held of the king as feudal superior, and the concept of allodial property did not exist.

ballybetagh: A unit of land division in Gaelic Ulster, supposed to contain 960 Irish acres. Like other similar land divisions, it was in fact a unit of assessment and not of mensuration and bore little or no relationship to actual area.

barony: The division of an Irish county, corresponding to the English 'hundred', and to the medieval Irish and Welsh 'cantred'.

betagh: (From Gaelic *Biatach*). In the Anglo-Norman system in Ireland the betaghs could be described as serfs of native Irish descent, bound to their lords and forbidden to leave their native place without permission. In the north of Ireland *biatach*, however, denoted persons of much higher status, the heads of minor landowning families.

black rent: A rent exacted without legal right, especially one paid in return for 'protection', i.e. to secure immunity from plunder or molestation.

bonnaght: (Gaelic *buannacht*). The wages and provisions of the galloglass, levied as a tax upon the country.

cantred: From the Welsh *Cantref*, the Cantred was the

administrative subdivision of the Anglo-Norman county, corresponding to the later barony.

Ceannfine: Anglicised 'Canfinny'. The head of a joint-family (*fine*) or clan in Irish law. Not to be confused with *ceannfeadhna*, which means simply a military leader.

clan: As defined in the text (Chapter I), 'a unilineal descent group forming a definite corporate entity with political and legal functions'.

coarb: Gaelic *Comharba*, Latin *Comorbanus* or *Converbius*. The coarb was literally the 'successor' of the patron saint, who as such enjoyed high spiritual prestige. The office was distinguished by this prestige rather than by any specific function. See Chapter V.

commendator: A person holding an abbey or priory *in commendam* by papal grant. Commendators were not members of the religious order to which their monastery belonged and were not, therefore, bound to adhere to its rule. They might often be in minor orders or even laymen.

coyne: Gaelic *Coinnmheadh*, meaning quartering or billeting. Used as a general term for all the various Irish exactions which consisted, at base, of the free quartering of the lord's soldiers and followers upon the country. See Chapter II.

creagh: Gaelic *Creach*. A cattle-raid or preying expedition. Not to be confused with *creaght* (q.v.)

creaght: (Also Kyrreaght etc.) The Anglicised form of the collective noun *Caoruigheacht* (pl. *Caoruigheachta*) meaning a herd of cattle with its keepers. It is often confused with *creagh* (q.v.) a cattle-raid.

cuddy: Gaelic *Cuid Oidhche*, (lit. night's portion). The entertainment (food, drink and lodging) which an Irish chief exacted for himself and his train from his subjects. See Chapter II.

erenagh: (Also Herenagh: Gaelic *Airchinneach*). The erenagh, in simplest terms, could be described as a hereditary tenant of church-lands, but he enjoyed a quasi-clerical status. See Chapter V. In late medieval times the word *Airchinneach*, in the southern half of Ireland, was also used to mean 'archdeacon'.

eric: The fine or compensation paid for homicide in Gaelic law, also called by English writers 'Saut'.

gavelkind: Properly, the system of inheritance to land which prevailed in Kent, by which all sons inherited in equal shares. The term was extended in English usuage (in strict usage, 'a custom in the nature of gavelkind') to denote the system of joint and equal inheritance among males found in Wales and Ireland and referred to here as 'Irish gavelkind'. See Chapter III.

heriot: The best animal owned by a tenant or vassal, which by custom the landlord or overlord was entitled to seize as a kind of 'death duty' on the tenant's death.

inquisition: An inquiry, by the evidence of witnesses, before a sworn jury, the normal method of ascertaining facts for legal purposes in the sixteenth and early seventeenth centuries. Also called in contemporary sources an 'Office'.

iraght: See *oireacht*.

liberty: A county or other area in which certain prerogatives of the crown connected with the administration of justice, etc., had been conceded to a private individual. Also called a franchise, or, in later times, a palatinate or county palatine.

marcher: Belonging to the marches, or frontier regions.

mark: An obsolete money of account, worth two-thirds of a pound, or 13s. 4d.

metayage: The system by which land is let and cultivated on the basis of a division of the crop between the landlord and the tenant. See Chapter VI.

nation: In sixteenth-century English usage a family, a body of persons sharing a common surname and descent.

noxial: Latin *Noctialis, noxalis*. The entertainment which an Irish bishop received from his erenaghs and other tenants and (sometimes) clergy, corresponding to the secular cuddy.

official: The title given to the judge of the diocesan court, who had jurisdiction in cases involving wills, marriage, etc.

oireacht: Anglicised Iraght, Eraght, etc. The primary meaning of this term was 'assembly', (for which *oireachtas* was the later term). In late medieval use *oireacht* denoted both the subjects and followers of a lord ('his Iraghts', in English usage) and the territory which he ruled. There seems to have been some confusion in English sources between *oireacht* and *uirrí* (q.v.). See Chapter II.

patrilineal: Reckoning descent or relationship *only* in the male line.

provisor: In the simplest terms, a person appointed ('provided') by the Pope to an ecclesiastical benefice.

sept: The normal term used by sixteenth and seventeenth century English writers for the basic Irish corporate family group. I have preferred to use the term clan (q.v.) as being in more general use. 'Sept' seems to be a translation of the Irish *Sliocht*, lit. 'a section'.

sláinte: The basic idea of this Irish word is that of 'guarantee' or 'indemnification'. In the later medieval period, it is used with the allied senses of (1) the protection extended by a greater man to a lesser one. (2) the suretyship of a third party for the observance of a contract. (3) the person extending such suretyship. The abstract noun is *slánuigheacht*.

tanist: Gaelic *Tánaiste* (occasionally *Táiniste*). Literally, 'second'. Usually used to denote the successor-designate of an Irish chief or lord, but occasionally used in its primary meaning of 'second in rank or position', without reference to succession. See Chapter II.

termon: Gaelic *Tearmonn*. The sanctuary lands attached to a church (though not all church-land was termon land). It enjoyed privileges of sanctuary and protection. The tenants of termon land were called termoners (Gaelic *tearmonnaigh*), which is thus a generic term for coarbs and erenaghs (q.q.v.).

tuarastal: A payment made to attach a person to the service of the giver. Sometimes large, it was on other occasions little more than symbolic. Acceptance of *tuarastal* involved acceptance of the superiority, or at least of the leadership, of the giver. Usually rendered in English as 'stipend'.

tuath: Latinised in the early period as *theodum* and *tuedum* and represented in Anglicised spelling by such forms as 'Tuogh' etc., the *tuath* was originally the small particular unit-state of the Gaelic system. The word became obsolete as a living term, probably in the thirteenth century, but remained a common constituent of the names of districts and even of single townlands, when these constituted in some ways units set apart from their neighbours, as, for instance, discrete portions of nearby lordships.

uirrí: Anglicised 'urriogh'. A vassal or sub-king.

unilineal: (Of descent groups) reckoning descent or relationship only in the male or only in the female line (*patrilineal* and *matrilineal* respectively).

References

[1] The definition of the clan and the remarks on its nature and functions draw largely on the discussion of the subject to be found in L. Krader, *Social Organization of the Mongol-Turkic pastoral Nomads,* 1963, 9 and 318ff., and in M. Fortes, *Kinship and the Social Order,* 1969, *passim*.

[2] G. I. Jones, 'Basutoland Medicine Murder', *H.M.S.O.*, [8209] (1951), quoted in Audrey I. Richards, 'African Chiefs and their Royal Relatives', *Royal Anthropological Institute Journal*, 91 (1961), 146.

[3] Printed in *Analecta Hibernica*, 3 (1931), pp. 62–150.

[4] *Miscellaneous Irish Annals*, ed. S. Ó hInnse, 1947, pp. 143–85.

[5] See P. MacCana, 'An Archaism in Irish Poetic Tradition', *Celtica*, 8 (1968), 179–81.

[6] 'The Lisgoole Agreement of 1580', ed. K. W. Nicholls, *Clogher Record*, 7 (1969), 27–33.

[7] That of 1421 is printed (with translation) as an appendix to K. W. Nicholls, 'The FitzMaurices of Kerry', *Kerry Archaeological Society Journal*, 3 (1970), 38–42. That of 1541 may be found in translated abstract in *Calendar of Ormond Deeds*, ed. Curtis, IV, 203–5.

Index

193